westermann

NOTTING HILL GATE

Workbook 6

Erarbeitet von:
Hanna Hoof (Schacht-Audorf), Theresa Künzel-Giller (Pforzheim),
Gabriele Linke (Marburg), Cedric Lütgert (Marburg),
Sascha Mohr (Wiesbaden), Maike Pegler (Sarstedt/Gödringen),
Sabina Piatzer (Hannover)

Fachliche Beratung:
Angela Berkenkamp (Wetzlar), Susanne Quandt (Bremen)

Notting Hill Gate 6
Workbook

Zusatzmaterialien zu Notting Hill Gate 6

Für Lehrkräfte:
- Textbook für Lehrkräfte 6 (ISBN 978-3-14-128285-6)
- Materialien für Lehrkräfte 6 (ISBN 978-3-14-128295-5)
- Lernerfolgskontrollen 6 (ISBN 978-3-14-128321-1)
- CD für Lehrkräfte 6 (ISBN 978-3-14-128305-1)
- DVD für Lehrkräfte 6 (ISBN 978-3-14-128315-0)
- Online-Diagnose zu Notting Hill Gate 6 www.onlinediagnose.de

Für Schülerinnen und Schüler:
- Textbook 6 (ISBN 978-3-14-128201-6)
- Interaktive Übungen 6 (WEB-14-128221)
- Arbeitsbuch Inklusion 6 (inkl. Audios) (ISBN 978-3-14-128231-3)
- Klassenarbeitstrainer 6 (ISBN 978-3-14-128247-4)
- Grammatiktrainer 6 (ISBN 978-3-14-128387-7)
- Wortschatztrainer 6 (ISBN 978-3-14-128241-2)

Das digitale Schulbuch und digitale Unterrichtsmaterialien für Schülerinnen und Schüler und für Lehrkräfte finden Sie in der BiBox – dem digitalen Unterrichtssystem passend zum Lehrwerk. Mehr Informationen über aktuelle Lizenzen finden Sie auf www.bibox.schule.

www.westermann.de/nhg

DIGITAL+

Alle digitalen Ergänzungen zum Buch erkennst du an dem Symbol **DIGITAL+**. Dazu zählen Audiotracks, Videoclips, Arbeitsblätter zur Medienbildung sowie die *Practise more*-Arbeitsblätter. Gehe auf **www.westermann.de/webcode** und gib den Webcode **WES-128211-001** ein. Du kannst auch den QR-Code scannen.

Redaktion: Jutta Eckardt-Scheurig
Illustrationen: Mario Ellert, Bremen
Umschlaggestaltung: LIO Design GmbH, Braunschweig
Layout: LIO Design GmbH, Braunschweig
Druck und Bindung: Westermann Druck GmbH, Georg-Westermann-Allee 66, 38104 Braunschweig

Das Arbeitsheft ist in zwei Varianten erhältlich:

Arbeitsheft
ISBN 978-3-14-**128211**-5
Druck A[1] / Jahr 2023

Arbeitsheft mit interaktiven Übungen
ISBN 978-3-14-**145259**-4
Druck A[1] / Jahr 2023

Alle Drucke der Serie A sind im Unterricht parallel verwendbar.

Inhaltsverzeichnis

In diesem Workbook findest du folgende Verweise und Arten von Aufgaben:

1 audio	Zu dieser Aufgabe gibt es einen Audiotrack, den du auch online abrufen kannst.
2 video	Zu dieser Aufgabe gibt es einen Videoclip, den du auch online abrufen kannst.
3 wordbank	In den Wordbanks im Textbook findest du Wörter nach Wortfeldern geordnet.
4 skill	Auf den Skills-Seiten im Textbook findest du Tipps und Strategien fürs Lernen.
5 grammar	Zu dieser Aufgabe gibt es Erklärungen im Grammatik-Teil des Textbooks.
6 media worksheet	Dieser Hinweis kennzeichnet Aufgaben, in denen du Medienkompetenz aufbaust und trainierst. Zu diesen Aufgaben gibt es Arbeitsblätter, die du über den Webcode oder den QR-Code auf Seite 2 abrufen kannst.
7 CHOOSE YOUR LEVEL	Bei diesen Aufgaben gibt es drei unterschiedliche Schwierigkeitsgrade: **I leicht II mittel III schwierig**
8 CHOOSE YOUR TASK	Hier gibt es drei Aufgaben, von denen du dir eine aussuchen kannst. Du kannst alleine, mit einem Partner oder einer Partnerin oder in einer Gruppe arbeiten.
DIGITAL+	Dieser Hinweis zeigt, dass es zusätzliches Material auf der Webseite gibt.
Practise reading	Hier erhältst du praktische Tipps, um deine Lesekompetenz zu schulen.
Challenge	So werden schwierige Zusatzaufgaben gekennzeichnet.
TARGET TASK SUPPORT	Hier findest du Hilfen zu den Target Tasks (Zielaufgaben) im Textbook.

Summer holidays

1a
grammar: simple past TB p. 174

Where were the children? Complete the sentences with words from the box.

1 George ________________ in the USA.

2 Sarah and her parents ________________ at an adventure park.

3 In Paris there ________________ so much to see.

4 David and his new friends ________________ at the seaside.

were · was · were · was

1b
grammar: simple past TB p. 174, wordbank: holidays p. 160

Read TB1b again and look at the photos. Write about them in your exercise book.

at the seaside · have fun · beach volleyball · water · mountains · sightseeing bus · in Paris · go hiking · fantastic view · an adventure park · nice weather

You can write:

In photo number 1 the boy is playing ...
He ...
In photo number 2 I can see ...
There is ...

1c

What do you like doing in the holidays? Rank the activities from 1 - 8.

- ☐ going to the swimming pool every day
- ☐ going on holiday
- ☐ seeing my grandparents
- ☐ sleeping in and playing computer games
- ☐ learning something new
- ☐ not doing anything
- ☐ travelling to where my parents are from
- ☐ riding my bike with my friends

Jason's summer holidays

2 CHOOSE YOUR LEVEL
audio 1/2

Listen to Jason and Zoe.

Tick ✓ the words you hear.

☐ summer camp → ☐ north → ☐ outside → ☐ beautiful

☐ boys and girls → ☐ teams → ☐ sunshine → ☐ brilliant

☐ best → ☐ favourite → ☐ guitar → ☐ swimming

II Tick ✓ true or false.

		true	false
1	Jason's holiday was terrible.		
2	He went to a summer camp for boys.		
3	The camp was in the north of England.		
4	There was a campfire every evening.		
5	At the campfire there was a boy with a guitar.		

III **Correct the false sentences in II in your exercise book.**

LANGUAGE HELP Die einfache Vergangenheit: verneinte Aussagen TB S. 175

Sätze im simple past verneinst du mit *didn't (did not)*. Das ist die Vergangenheitsform von *don't* und *doesn't* und ist in allen Personen gleich. Das Verb selbst bleibt im Infinitiv, weil *didn't* die Verneinung schon anzeigt.

bejaht: *Charlie went to London. He visited a museum.* verneint: *Charlie didn't go to London. He didn't visit a museum.*

Ava and Tarek's holidays

3 grammar: simple past TB p. 174-175

What did Ava and Tarek do in the holidays? What didn't they do? Write sentences in your exercise book.

	Ava	Tarek
+	be in Poland visit grandma have a lazy horse have fun be happy	be in Wales arrive on Friday milk a cow go cycling make fresh milkshakes
–	be in London stay at a hotel go to a museum play computer games be sad	be in Italy say that farms are boring be afraid of cows be in Wales with his uncle feed the cows

A farm holiday

4 grammar: simple past TB p. 174-175

Write about Tarek's farm holiday. Use the simple past.

+ ~~play~~ · learn · write · ...

– ~~go~~ · read · sit · feed · ...

~~with a cat~~ · the pigs · to bake cakes · a diary · a book · for long walks · in the grass · ...

Tarek played with a cat. He didn't go

Simple past

5 grammar: simple past TB p. 174

Write down the simple past. Add the correct simple present forms. Check the spelling in your dictionary.

~~stayed~~ · took · went · learnt · loved · spent · played · made · stood · ate · had · visited

stayed – stay ______

took – ______

______

______

Karen's fantastic holidays

6a CHOOSE YOUR LEVEL grammar: simple past TB p. 174, wordbank: holidays TB p. 160

I Complete the yellow part of the letter. II Complete the yellow and the green part of the letter.
III Complete the letter. In the orange part, write about a shopping trip to Vienna[1]. Then finish the letter.

Dear Grandpa, how are you? Today is the last day of our holiday in Austria[2]. We ______ (have) so much fun! The weather ______ (is) perfect. We ______ (have) lots of great food. On the first day, Anthony and I ______ (go) bobsleighing[3]. We ______ (love) it. It ______ (is) so exciting!

On most days, we all ______ (hike) in the mountains. The views ______ (are) fantastic. When we ______ (are) hungry, we ______ (have) lunch in mountain hut[4].

______

______

______

1 Vienna – Wien, 2 **Austria** – Österreich, 3 **bobsleighing** – Bobfahren, **4 mountain hut** – Berghütte

6b grammar: simple past questions TB p. 176

Write questions for the answers.

1 ______ They were in Austria

2 ______ Yes, they had a lot of fun.

3 ______ The weather was great.

4 ______ They had lunch in a mountain hut.

Practise reading

Tipps 1 und 2

1 Bevor du einen Text liest, sieh dir die Überschrift an und überlege, worum es gehen könnte.
2 Wenn es zu einem Text Bilder gibt, sieh sie dir an. Sie können dir Hinweise auf den Inhalt geben.

Back in Notting Hill

7a

Look at the title of this text. What do you expect? Tick ✓ .

I expect a text about ... ☐ a holiday. ☐ a tour of Notting Hill. ☐ a weekend away.

7b

Look at the pictures. What do they show? Take notes or write sentences.

1

2

3

7c

Read the text. Can you find the information you expected in 7a?
Underline it. Then circle the words in the text that match the pictures.

Ava: Lily, your new room looks amazing! You have so much space now.

Harry: And so do I. No more socks everywhere ... Tarek, how were the last days of your holiday in Wales?

Tarek: After our week on the farm, my dad and I went to Cardiff for a couple of days. It was great. We went to Cardiff Castle and the Welsh Folk Museum.

Lily: What was that like?

Tarek: The Welsh Folk Museum is an open-air museum. There is a roundhouse, for example, that shows how people lived two thousand years ago. Look, I've got a picture. There's also an old school, a hotel, old shops and lots of old farmhouses.

Ava: And how did you like the castle? What did you do there?

Tarek: We went on a tour of the castle. At first I thought it would be boring, but the guide was really cool. Did you know that the Romans first built a fort there? Later the Normans came and built the castle.

Lily: Thank you for the history lesson, Tarek. Did you learn any words in Welsh?

Tarek: Yes, I did. But I found Welsh really difficult. For example, Wales is "Cymru" in Welsh. And "Good morning" is "Bore da". But there are also harder words, like "Shwmae" – that's "Hello".

Harry: Wow! That sounds difficult to me.

PRACTISE READING

Haben **Tipps 1 und 2** dir geholfen, den Text zu verstehen? ◯ ja ◯ teilweise ◯ nein

Lily's new room

8a audio 1/7

Look at picture 1. Listen and repeat the words.

8b

Do you remember Harry and Lily's old bedroom? There is a picture of it on page 96. Look at the three pictures. What is different? What is new? Describe the rooms. Make notes.

8c CHOOSE YOUR LEVEL media worksheet 5

Use your notes to talk about the rooms. Record yourself. Edit your recording.

You can say:

I can see ... *There aren't any ...*
There are ... *Now Lily has got ...*
... is big / small / nice / ...

- **Talk about the pictures for 40 seconds.**
- **Talk about the pictures for 60 seconds.**
- **Talk about the pictures for 90 seconds.**

1

2

Ellen's holiday

9 CHOOSE YOUR TASK audio 1/8, skill: listening TB p. 151

Listen to TB7b again and take notes.

A **Write speech bubbles for the pictures.**

B **Write a dialogue for one of the pictures. Write it in your exercise book.**

C **Create a scene from Ellen's holidays. Draw it, use figures or act it out. You can make a video.**

Sound check

10a audio 1/9

Listen to the words and repeat them.

milked · needed · moved ·
booked · waited · renovated · laughed
decided · cycled · lived · happened

10b

Listen again and fill in the lists.

/-t/	/-d/	/-ɪd/
milked	*moved*	*needed*

10c audio 1/10

Listen again and check your lists.

Everybody's holiday

11 CHOOSE YOUR LEVEL audio 1/8, skill: reading TB p. 154

What did everyone do in the holidays? Complete the fact files for Ava, Tarek, Uncle Sami and Ellen.
I Choose two of the fact files. II Choose three of the fact files. III Complete the fact files.

Ava (TB p. 9, 2a)	Tarek (TB p. 9, 2a and p. 12, 6b)
Where:	Where:
Who with:	Who with:
What:	What:
Fun fact:	Fun fact:
Uncle Sami (TB p. 10, 3a)	Ellen (TB p. 13, 7b)
Where:	Where:
Who with:	Who with:
What:	What:
Fun fact:	Fun fact:

My amazing holiday

12

Complete the diary entry with words from the box.

~~busy~~ · plane · by the seaside · cows · chickens · yesterday · space[1] ·
thousand · tomorrow · difficult · tasted delicious · strange · unfortunately

1 space – Weltraum

Dear diary, This summer was very *busy* . I wanted to travel to ______ to see the view but finding a flight was ______ . So I spent a week ______ . But I didn't stay in England. I took a ______ to the USA. ______ I didn't meet my relatives there. They were on holiday in England. :-(At the airport I met a ______ lady. She invited me to her farm in Scotland. So after my holiday I travelled a ______ kms to visit her. In the morning I went riding. Afterwards I sat in the grass, fed the ______ and milked the ______ . The fresh milk ______ . I had a lot of fun. So ______ I moved to Scotland. And ______ it's back to work. Phew! What a busy holiday!

Challenge: Rewrite the diary entry. Use your own words to complete the text.

A holiday video

13a

video 1, skill: watching a video clip TB p. 156, media worksheet 1

Watch the video clip in TB10a again. Who did what? Match the names: Lilly, Lewis and Maria.

______ - *went abroad* - *went to the beach every day* - *saw lots of family* - *mum comes from Sweden*[1] **1 Sweden** – Schweden	______ - *went abroad with mum and sisters* - *played in the pool a lot* - *relaxed and listened to music*	______ - *didn't go abroad* - *went to the beach sometimes* - *went swimming in a friend's pool* - *played computer games*

13b

Fill in these notes for the other children. Use the phrases from the box.

went on holiday in the south of England · ate lots of Spanish food · went to Spain · stayed in a hotel near the beach · it was sunny and windy · went on long walks

Chloe - *went to Grimsby* - - *visited grandparents*	______ - - - - *holiday was really nice*	______ - - - *went camping* -

Rent a bike

14 CHOOSE YOUR LEVEL

skill: mediation TB p. 155

Deine Eltern wollen im Peak District Fahrrad fahren gehen und die Räder dort ausleihen, aber sie verstehen die Informationen auf der Webseite nicht. Schau dir die Webseite an und beantworte ihre Fragen auf Deutsch. Mache dir Notizen und nimm deine Antworten auf.

I Answer two of the questions.
II Answer three of the questions.
III Answer the questions.

1 Muss man die Räder online reservieren oder können wir da einfach so welche bekommen?
2 Wie kann man denn herausfinden, wie teuer das wird?
3 Was muss man da mitbringen?
4 Wann ist der Laden geöffnet?
5 Wann machen die abends zu?

BOB'S BIKE SHOP

Booking
Online booking is recommended. Walk-in hires are welcome, but will be served on a first-come-first-serve basis.

Prices
We have a range of flexible pricing for all cycling needs. Please check www.peakdistrict.gov.uk/bikeprices

Checklist
To hire your bike, please bring with you the following:
- A cash deposit that will be refunded on return of the bike
- Proof of identity: Photo ID required (driving licence or passport)

Opening hours
Open every day between March and October from 9:30am. Closing times depend on how busy we are.

My holiday post TARGET TASK SUPPORT

15 media worksheet 2, wordbank: holidays TB p. 160, skill: writing TB p. 153

1 Use the word web to organize your ideas for your blog post.

activities

people

weather

what was special

places

ideas for my blog post

2 Complete the sentences with your ideas. Choose the sentences you want to use in your blog post. First, find a good title for your blog post.

Fresh fish / ______________________

Hi, I'm ______________________ and I want to tell you about my amazing holiday in *Greece*[1] / ______________________, because it was *very special* / ______________________.

A great experience was *eating fresh fish straight from a fishing boat* / ______________________.

I really liked *the traditional dance Sirtaki* / ______________________.

A funny thing happened *one night* / ______________________.

After dinner, people threw their dishes[2] *on the floor and danced on them* / ______________________.

It was brilliant to *watch* / ______________________.

I also really liked the *language* / ______________________.

I recommend *learning a few words* / ______________________ before going to *Greece* / ______________________.

If you like, please leave a comment[3] under my blog post. Thank you very much!

1 Greece – Griechenland, **2 dishes** – Geschirr, **3 comment** – Kommentar

3 Match ⁄ the sentence halves to create polite comments. You can use them to comment on your classmates' posts.

1 Your blog post is
2 I liked
3 Could you please
4 I think your blog post is
5 You could
6 Your blog post really makes me want
7 I don't think

to visit / to go to / find out more about ...!
tell us more about ...
that's a good idea.
write more about / add more ... to make it better.
really interesting / fascinating / brilliant / ...
a bit boring / too short / very complicated / ...
the way you described your adventure holiday.

Tipp: Einen Blogpost kommentieren

Wenn du einen Blog kommentierst, solltest du immer höflich bleiben und negative Aussagen möglichst vermeiden. Zum Beispiel ist "I think that's a bad idea." eher unhöflich. Besser wäre "I don't think that's a good idea." Außerdem sind "please" und "thank you" echte Höflichkeitshelfer, die du häufig verwenden solltest, z.B. "Could you please write some more about this interesting topic? Thank you!"

Talking about London

1

What comes to mind when you think about London? Talk about your ideas.

the King · London is very big · red buses · cool · there is a nice big park · exciting · Sherlock Holmes · there are many people · many museums · you can take great photos · ...

You can say:
I think of ...
I think it is ...
I know that ...
I heard that ...
I saw a film about ...
I believe that ...

More about the sights

2 CHOOSE YOUR TASK

A: media worksheet 4

Look at TB1 again.

A **Find out how old the sights are. You can make a timeline.**
B **Make an acrostic with the letters LONDON.**
C **Write down quiz questions about London for a partner.**

A

Buckingham Palace 1703
1828 London Zoo
Big Ben 1843
1881 The Natural History Museum
The London Eye 1999
2014 The Sky Garden

LANGUAGE HELP

Die Steigerung von Adjektiven mit more und most TB S.177

Mehrsilbige Adjektive werden mit *more* und *most* gesteigert. Du stellst dabei more oder most vor das Adjektiv. Das Adjektiv selbst bleibt unverändert. Beispiel: Adjektiv *interesting* Komparativ *more interesting* Superlativ *most interesting*

Wenn du Dinge miteinander vergleichen willst, benutzt du *more than* und *the most*.
Beispiel: *The red T-shirt is more expensive than the blue T-shirt. The yellow T-shirt is the most expensive.*

The most useful fact files

3a

Read the fact files about London sights.

POPULAR SIGHTS

The National History Museum:
Visitors: 4.62 million
The Tower of London:
Visitors: 2.74 million
The British Museum:
Visitors: 6.42 million
The Science Museum:
Visitors: 3,35 million

TICKET PRICES

The Tower of London:
Adult: £29.90 Child: £14.90
Tower Bridge:
Adult: £10.30 Child: £5.30
The London Eye:
Adult: £33.50 Child: £30.00
Madame Tussauds:
Adult: £39.00 Child: £35.50

NEAR A TUBE STATION

The Tower of London:
0,1 miles from the station
Madame Tussauds:
0,1 miles from the station
The British Museum:
0,3 miles from the station
Buckingham Palace:
0,4 miles from the station

3b CHOOSE YOUR LEVEL grammar: comparison of adjectives TB p.177

Write about the sights and compare them. Use the information in 3a and your own opinion.
Write four sentences. Write six sentences. Write eight sentences.

popular · boring · interesting · cheap · expensive · near · close · famous · fun

is an expensive sight in London.

is closer to a Tube station than

is more popular than

Something else about London

4a video 2, media worksheet 1

Watch the video clip in TB4b again. In which order do you hear the sentences or sentence parts?

A Not far from Buckingham Palace is Hyde Park.
B Many people think that the tower is called Big Ben.
C The London Eye, one of the tallest ferris wheels in the world.
D The castle is more than 900 years old.
E You can visit some of the 775 rooms.

1	C
2	
3	
4	
5	

4b CHOOSE YOUR LEVEL

Watch the video clip. Listen to the sights. Answer question 1 questions 1 and 2 the questions.

1 Which of the sights can you see on the map in your TB on page 21?

2 Name three sights that are not on the map in your TB on page 21.

3 Write two or more sentences about one of the sights that are on the map but are not mentioned in the video.

Challenge: **Plan a day in London for you and your friends. Where do you want to go? Write about it.**

Tube announcements

5 audio 1/13

Listen to the different announcements on the Tube. Number the pictures in the correct order.

☐ 

☐ 
☐ 

☐ 
☐ 

Sights along the way

6a audio 1/14, skill: listening TB p. 151

Listen to TB6a again. Number the sights in the order you hear them.

- ☐ Parliament Street
- ☐ Big Ben
- ☐ Queen Victoria Memorial
- ☐ Westminster Bridge
- ☐ Birdcage Walk
- ☐ Winston Churchill Statue
- ☐ St James's Park

6b

Listen again and answer the questions.

1 Where does the family go first?

2 Which bridge do they have to cross?

3 What can they see on their left?

4 What is on their right all the time?

5 Which memorial is on Spur Road?

6c

Listen to the man. How often does he say … ?

walk along	/
walk on until	//
turn right	
cross	
on your left	
go straight on	
walk past	
on your right	

Walk straight on

7a audio 1/15

Listen to the directions and repeat them.

7b

Listen again. Do the moves that go with the directions.

Another sight

8

Complete Ellen's text message with the correct numbers.

1 under · 2 six · 3 more interesting · 4 older · 5 today · 6 hope · 7 walk · 8 uniform · 9 old

Ellen Hi Mum, It's us again. How are you?
5 we are on a history tour. We went to Tower Bridge first. It is a very _ bridge and it was exciting to _ on it. Sometimes ships go _ the bridge. Now we are at the Tower of London. It is even _ than Tower Bridge and much _ . 😉 The Beefeaters are wearing a special _. I _ we can see the ravens, too. There are at least _ ravens at the Tower of London.
Talk to you later! Bye, Ellen and Nick
11:21am

Sarah's favourite sights

9 CHOOSE YOUR LEVEL

audio 1/16, skill: listening TB p. 151

Listen to TB9a again.

I 1 Circle the sights you hear.

Tower Bridge · the London Eye · the Museum of London · the Bank of England · Elizabeth Tower · Covent Garden · Madame Tussauds · King's Cross Station

2 Underline the correct sentence endings.

Sarah talks about museums / shopping / Buckingham Palace.

In the afternoon, the children go to a museum / King's Cross Station / Madame Tussauds.

II Answer the questions.

1 Who really likes museums?

2 Who wants to go to platform 9¾?

3 Where do the children get their ideas for their day out in London?

4 Why do the children decide to go to Covent Garden?

III Answer the questions. You can also use the texts on p. 24 in your textbook for help.

1 What are the children's plans for the morning and the afternoon?

2 Why do the children decide to go to Covent Garden? Give two reasons.

3 Why do the children decide not to go to Madame Tussauds?

4 What is special about platform 9¾ ?

Challenge: **Make a list of museums you can recommend to Sarah and say why they are interesting.**

Practise reading

Tipps 6 und 10

6 Versuche, dir die Wörter, die du nicht gleich verstehst, aus dem Textzusammenhang oder aus der Situation zu erschließen. Nutze dabei nicht nur dein Allgemeinwissen, sondern auch deine sprachlichen Vorkenntnisse.
10 Wenn du genaue Informationen in einem Text finden willst, kannst du ihn gezielt nach und nach durchgehen. Diese Fragen können dir helfen: Wo? / **Where?** Wann? / **When?** Was? / **What?** Wie? / **How?** Wer / **Who?**

Tower Bridge

10a

Look at the picture and the title of the flyer. Tick ✓ what you expect.

- ☐ a walk to the Tower of London
- ☐ a walk across a glass floor
- ☐ a walk through London

10b

Read the questions and the flyer. Underline the information. Then answer the questions.

1 Where is the sight?

2 When can you visit it?

3 What is special about Tower Bridge?

4 How high is the glass floor walkway?

5 How much are the tickets?

6 How can you get there?

Did you know that you can walk on a glass floor high up inside Tower Bridge? Through the floor, you have a fantastic view of London below. The glass floor walkway is 42 metres above the River Thames and 33.5 metres above the road. We hope you're not afraid of heights! Entry is £10.60 for adults and £5.30 for children. The Bridge is open to visitors every day from 9.30am to 6pm. Our address is Tower Bridge Road, London, SE1 2UP. The nearest Tube station is Tower Hill. You can take the District and Circle lines to get here.

PRACTISE READING

Haben **Tipps 6 und 10** dir geholfen, den Text zu verstehen? ◯ ja ◯ teilweise ◯ nein

What's the best?

11 grammar: the comparison of adjectives TB p.177

Complete the sentences with the correct words.

good (3x) · better (3x) · the best (3x)

1 ________ sight in London is Tower Bridge. My friend says the London Eye is ________ . I don't know, but it is ________ , too. 2 One of my favourite activities in London is going to the indoor skate park BaySixty6. I think it's really ________ . My dad says ________ activity is walking along the river. I'm not sure but it is ________ than shopping. 3 I like lasagna, it's really ________ . But spaghetti is even ________ . And my favourite food is fish and chips. Yes, I think fish and chips are ________ .

Sound check

12a audio 1/18

Listen and repeat the words.

~~parliament~~ · expensive · yesterday · attraction · comparative · entertainment · combination · popular · exhibition · comparison

12b

Where is the stress? Sort the words into the lists. Underline the stressed syllables[1].

1st syllable	2nd syllable	3rd syllable
parliament		

12c audio 1/19

Listen and check your lists.

A London quiz

13a

What do you know about London? Tick ✓ the correct answers.

1 Buckingham Palace is	☐ a museum.	☐ a hotel	☐ the home of the royal family
2 The Natural History Museum is	☐ where you can find out about dinosaurs.	☐ a park in London.	☐ where you can listen to stories.
3 Covent Garden is	☐ the name of the transport museum.	☐ a popular shopping area with street cafés.	☐ a very big flower shop.
4 Big Ben is	☐ the name of a famous bell.	☐ a tall clock tower.	☐ a very tall person.
5 Sky Garden is	☐ the tallest building in London.	☐ a famous park with a garden.	☐ a café and restaurant on a skyscraper.
6 The London Eye is	☐ an old cinema.	☐ a ferris wheel with a great view of London.	☐ a very famous bridge.

1 **stressed syllable** – betonte Silbe

13b CHOOSE YOUR LEVEL
wordbank: getting around TB p. 162

Write more quiz questions for a partner in your exercise book. You can use ideas from the box.
I Write two quiz questions. II Write three quiz questions. III Write five quiz questions.

London Zoo · the Tower of London · platform 9¾ · Madame Tussauds · Tower Bridge glass floor walkway · Wembley Stadium · ...

A cable car ride

14
skill: mediation TB p. 155

Du bist in London in einer Touristeninformation. Eine deutsche Familie hat Schwierigkeiten, die Broschüre „Emirates Air Line cable car" zu verstehen. Lies die Broschüre und beantworte ihre Fragen auf Deutsch.

I Answer three of the questions.
II Answer five of the questions.
III Answer the questions.

1 Über welchen Fluss fahren die Gondeln? ____________
2 Wie viele Gondeln gibt es? ____________
3 Was sieht man während der Fahrt? ____________
____
4 Wie viel kostet ein Einzelticket? ____________
5 Wie lange dauert die Überfahrt? ____________
6 Wie viele Menschen passen in eine Gondel? ____________
7 Wo kann man ein- und aussteigen? ____________
____

Emirates Air Line cable car

Glide above the River Thames in one of the 34 gondolas of the Emirates Air Line cable car and take in the spectacular view.

What can I see?
Enjoy beautiful views of the Thames, London's skyline, the Greenwich Peninsula, the Royal Docks and the O2 Arena.

How much is a journey?
Buy single tickets for £6.00 and return tickets for £8.00. You can also buy a multi-journey boarding pass for 10 single trips on the Emirates Air Line cable car for £17.

How long does the Emirates cable car journey take?
The Emirates cable car journey times are adjusted according to passenger flow and weather conditions and range from 5 to around 10 minutes.

How many people can ride in one gondola?
There is a maximum capacity for ten passengers per gondola.

Where can I take the cable cars from/to?
You can take the Emirates Air Line cable cars from North Greenwich or from the Royal Victoria side of the river.

Above the Thames

15a

Read the flyer in WB14 again and look at this picture. Imagine you are in the gondola that is passing the O2 Arena. Make notes.

15b
media worksheet 5

Use your notes to talk about the ride. Talk for one minute or longer. Record yourself. Edit your recording.

You can say:
I am in a ... I took the ... from ... The view is ...
I can see ... There are ... There is also ...
The ticket costs ... I really ... because ...

A day out in London TARGET TASK SUPPORT

16 media worksheet 4, wordbank: getting around TB p. 162

1 Decide on your perfect day out in London.

My page for a travel guide for a day out in London is for: ______

2 Fill in the word web. Collect ideas from the Internet or use the webcode.

activities
time of day
places
prices
how to get there
ideas for my travel guide page
interesting sights

3 Now complete the sentences to get a draft.

In the morning:

Why not start your cool day out with ______

It's a lot of fun to ______

You can get there ______ *It costs* ______

At lunchtime:

Why not go to ______

After that, take a walk ______

In the afternoon:

Don't miss ______

You could also ______

______ *is an exciting thing to do.*

In the evening:

Travel to ______ *and see* ______.

Enjoy the ______

Tipp: Welche Informationen findet man in einem Reiseführer für eine Stadt?

Die meisten Reiseführer bieten ihren Lesern folgende Informationen an:

- Einen Überblick über die Stadt mit den verschiedenen Stadtteilen und was es dort Besonderes gibt.
- Informationen über das Klima: Zu welcher Jahreszeit kann man mit welchen Temperaturen rechnen?
- Wie bewegt man sich fort? Gibt es U-Bahnen oder ein gut ausgebautes Busnetz? Kann man die Stadt gut zu Fuß erkunden?
- Welche Sehenswürdigkeiten sollte man unbedingt anschauen? Welche sind kostenlos?
- Welche der teuren Attraktionen lohnen sich wirklich? Was kostet der Eintritt und wie kommt man hin?
- Wo kann man am besten übernachten und wo gibt es richtig gutes Essen? Gibt es Spezialitäten?

Die Check out-Seiten helfen dir einzuschätzen, was du schon gut kannst und was du noch üben solltest.
Löse die Aufgaben auf dieser Doppelseite und male die Kreise wie bei einer Ampel rot, gelb oder grün aus.

Rot: Das kann ich noch nicht.

Gelb: Das fällt mir noch schwer.

Grün: Das kann ich gut.

1 Kannst du verstehen, was jemand über seine Ferien berichtet?
2 Kannst du von Ereignissen in der Vergangenheit erzählen?
3 Kannst du jemandem Fragen über die vergangenen Ferien stellen?
4 Kannst du Sehenswürdigkeiten in London beschreiben?
5 Kannst du Personen oder Dinge vergleichen?
6 Kannst du jemandem eine Wegbeschreibung geben?

1 audio 1/20

Listen to Poppy telling her neighbour Lola about her holidays. Tick the right answers.

1 Where did Poppy go in the holidays?	☐ to Ireland	☐ to Scotland	☐ to Holland
2 What was her favourite place in Edinburgh?	☐ the castle	☐ the Old Town	☐ the Science Centre
3 How long did she stay in Edinburgh?	☐ for three days	☐ for four days	☐ for one week
4 Where did she go after that?	☐ to a lake	☐ to a farm	☐ to a village
5 What was the weather like?	☐ It was rainy.	☐ It was sunny.	☐ It was cloudy.

Ich kann verstehen, was jemand über seine Ferien berichtet. ○

2 grammar: simple past positive statements TB p. 174

Write about the children's activities in the holidays.

1 Arlo: cycle with his friends on sunny days ______

2 Lola: visit her aunt in Spain for two weeks ______

3 Tonya: often help her parents in their shop ______

4 Abdul: paint his room, read a lot of comics ______

Ich kann von Ereignissen in der Vergangenheit erzählen. ○

3 grammar: simple past questions TB p. 176

Ivy asks Logan about his holidays. Unscramble her questions.

1 fun · you · Wales · Did · have · in · ? ______

2 stay · How · there · did · you · long · ? ______

3 to · Did · beach · go · you · the · ? ______

4 did · holidays · else · do · you · your · in · What · ? ______

Ich kann jemandem Fragen über die vergangenen Ferien stellen. ○

4

Use the facts to write about Hyde Park.

Hyde Park
- large park in London
- many attractions
- large lake called the Serpentine
- beautiful flower gardens
- more than 3,000 trees
- fun activities, examples:
  - do sports (football, tennis, yoga, ...)
  - rent boat
  - go to music events

Ich kann Sehenswürdigkeiten in London beschreiben.

5 grammar: comparison of adjectives TB p. 177

Write comparisons.

1 small: rabbits – hamsters – bees
2 tall: cows – horses – dinosaurs
3 young: teenagers – children – babies
4 expensive: skateboards – bikes – cars

1 *Rabbits are small. Hamsters are* ______ *. Bees are* ______
2 ______
3 ______
4 ______

Ich kann Personen und Dinge vergleichen.

6 media worksheet 5

You are at the station. A woman asks you the way to the castle. Give her directions. Make a recording.

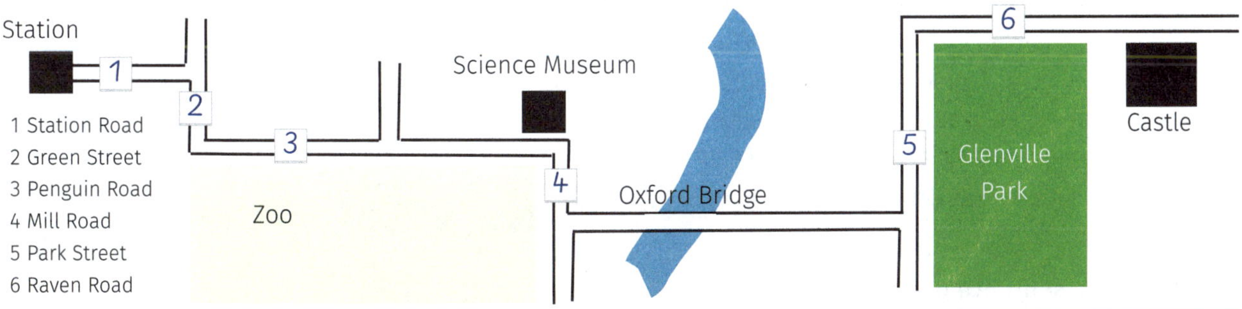

Ich kann jemandem eine Wegbeschreibung geben.

Wenn du noch mehr üben möchtest, gehe zu Practise more – Unit 1. DIGITAL+

Festival words

1 grammar: simple present TB p. 178

Talk about the festivals you know.

You can say:
I know …
We celebrate … in winter.
In my family, we …
I really like to celebrate …
My grandparents always …
… is a festival of lights.
There is special food at …
My favourite festival of the year is …

More about the festivals

2 audio 1/21

Listen to the children. Number the festivals in the correct order.

- ☐ Eid
- ☐ Hanukkah
- ☐ Diwali
- ☐ Easter
- ☐ Chinese New Year

Challenge: **Read about Hanukkah in TB1c again. Listen to the boy talking about Hanukkah. Which information do you hear that is new? Take notes.**

What people do to celebrate

3 CHOOSE YOUR LEVEL grammar: simple present TB p. 178

I Read the text.

Every year in December, many people around the world celebrate Christmas. On Christmas Eve, our family goes to church, and we watch a play which tells the story of the birth[1] of Jesus Christ. After church, we go home and have a big meal. Our whole family is there, and we have a lot of fun together. Grandpa always tells funny stories from the past. On Christmas morning, we find our presents under the Christmas tree.

1 **birth** – Geburt

Underline the correct words.

1 On Christmas Eve/On Christmas morning, the family goes to church.
2 The family listens to a concert/watches a play in church.
3 Grandma/Grandpa tells funny stories from the past.
4 The children find the presents under the Christmas tree/under the table.

II Read the text.

Our family is from India, and we have a great and very colourful festival: the Holi Festival. During the Holi Festival we celebrate the beginning of spring. People come together and throw coloured powder[1] and water into the air. Then all the people are coloured[2] in the colours of the rainbow[3]. The colour goes everywhere. Don't wear any clothes you want to keep afterwards! We usually celebrate the Holi Festival in March. The date depends on the moon. Sometimes it takes place at the end of February.

1 **coloured powder** – Farbpulver, 2 **are coloured** – sind gefärbt, 3 **rainbow** – Regenbogen

Match ╱ the sentence parts.

1 People from India have the Holi Festival
2 During the Holi Festival
3 The Holi Festival usually
4 After the Holi Festival

people are coloured in all the colours of the rainbow.
you can throw away your clothes.
to celebrate the beginning of spring.
takes place in March.

III Read the text.

In Mexico, we have a special tradition. It is called Día De Los Muertos – the Day of the Dead. It sounds a little bit scary, but it is a huge and cool festival. It takes place on October 31 every year and lasts for three days! It is so much fun! We dress up as skeletons and paint our faces. It is a little bit like the American Halloween. But we celebrate the Day of the Dead as a family. There are also a lot of flowers. We believe that on this day the souls[1] of our family members come down from heaven[2] and live with us again for 24 hours. So I can show my great-grandfather what I can do on my skateboard.

1 soul – Seele, **2 heaven** – Himmel

Complete the sentences.

1 The Day of the Dead takes place ______

2 It sounds scary, but it is ______

3 People dress up ______

4 This festival is a bit like ______

Celebration words

4

Find the celebration words in the word snake and sort them into the table.

TRADITIONAL | BELIEVEFESTIVALCELEBRATECOSTUMERELIGIOUSDECORATEDANCER

verbs	adjectives	nouns
	traditional	

All over the world

5

audio 1/22, wordbank: celebrations TB p. 163

Listen to TB4b again and underline the correct sentence parts.

1 The Chinese celebrate New Year in January or February / March or April / November or December and the celebration lasts 15 / 18 / 25 days.

2 Farida tells us that in India people celebrate New Year's many times in the year / on different days / never. She celebrates New Year on December 31 / January 1 / January 31.

3 In Scotland / Spain / England, there is the tradition of first footing. The first / second / last person to come to your house in the new year is the bringer of good luck.

4 Paola speaks about New Year's in Spain. In the evening / at 12 o'clock at night / in the morning, you have to eat two / six / twelve grapes for good luck.

Let's celebrate

6a audio 1/23

Listen to the people. What are they saying? Do you understand any of the languages?

6b

Can you say it in other languages? Make a class recording.

Last New Year's Eve

7a wordbank: celebrations TB p. 163

What did you do last New Year's Eve? Write your name into the table. Read the questions and tick ✓.

Did you ...	Your name:	Name:	Name:	Name:
celebrate with your family?				
watch the fireworks?				
have a party?				
go to a party?				
stay up until midnight?				
...				
...				

7b

Ask three classmates about their New Year's Eve. Write their names into the table and tick their anwers.

7c CHOOSE YOUR LEVEL

Write a short report about your classmates' answers in your exercise book.
I Write three sentences or more. II Write six sentences or more. III Write nine sentences or more.

You can write:

One of the children celebrated ... Two of us watched ... No one had ... One person ... All of us ...

Sound check

8a audio 1/24

Learn to say the letter 'r'. Listen to the words and repeat them.

8b

Listen again and write the words in your exercise book.

8c

Check the spelling of the words in the dictionary in your textbook.

Chinese New Year

9 CHOOSE YOUR LEVEL media worksheet 5

Du hast ein Plakat gesehen mit einer Einladung zum Chinesischen Neujahrsfest. Jetzt möchtest du deinen englischen Freunden davon erzählen. Was sagst du? Mache dir Notizen und nimm dich auf. Berichte von I drei Details II fünf Details III sieben Details.

You can say:

I saw an invitation for a … celebration.
It is on …
It starts … with …
After that the parents …

Your Halloween word web

10 wordbank: celebrations TB p. 163

Start a Halloween word web. Collect more words and phrases as you learn more about Halloween. Have a look at pages 36-39 in your textbook.

Halloween tasks

11 CHOOSE YOUR TASK A: audio 1/25 B: media worksheet 4

A **Listen to the girl. What was her costume? She was a ____________. Draw the costume.**
B **What do children in the USA do to celebrate Halloween? Find out and tell the class.**
C **Make a Halloween word search or word puzzle for a partner.**

Practise reading

Tipps 3 und 7
3 Beim Lesen von kürzeren Texten kannst du alle bekannten Wörter unterstreichen. Manchmal erkennst du noch mehr Wörter, wenn du dir den Text anhörst. Alle unbekannten Wörter, die dir wichtig erscheinen, solltest du nachschlagen.
7 Es gibt viele Wörter, die im Englischen und im Deutschen ähnlich oder sogar gleich sind. Es kann dir helfen, nach solchen Wörtern zu suchen, wenn du einen Text liest.

Halloween today – opinions

12a audio 1/26

Read the texts and underline all the words you know. Now listen to the texts and underline the words you recognize[1] when you hear them.

1 **recognize** – erkennen

Jessica, 14: Halloween is only about spending money. You have to buy costumes, decorations, sweets, ... It's so commercial. I don't think that's cool!

Tom, 13: For my family, 31 October is still the Christian holiday of All Hallows' Eve. I think Halloween is stupid. Dressing up in scary costumes is for little children and I don't like going to people's houses and asking them for sweets. I don't like Halloween!

Liam, 12: I love Halloween! It's fun to dress up in scary costumes and go around the neighbourhood to collect sweets. You say: "trick or treat". That means that you ask people to give you sweets or you play funny tricks on them. My favourite costume is the mummy. You just have to wrap yourself in toilet paper and that's it!

Christopher, 14: Halloween is great! Why? Because you can be a really scary character, eat lots of sweets and do all kinds of fun games like apple bobbing, or you can carve jack-o'-lanterns out of pumpkins.
My cousin John lives in the USA. Halloween is huge there! One day, I want to go to New York and watch the Halloween parade!

12b

Circle all the words that are like German words you know. Make a list.

English word	German word

English word	German word

PRACTISE READING

Haben **Tipps 3 und 7** dir geholfen, den Text zu verstehen? ◯ ja ◯ teilweise ◯ nein

Your opinion

13 CHOOSE YOUR LEVEL

media worksheet 5

Read the children's statements in TB7b again. Compare them to your notes in TB7d. Say what you think. Record yourself and edit the recording.

I Talk for 30 seconds or longer.
II Talk for 40 seconds or longer.
III Talk for 60 seconds or longer.

You can say:

Jessica thinks that Halloween …
I agree with her. I think that …
Liam says … but I think …
I don't think that …
I don't agree with … because

Halloween poems and rhymes

14a

audio 1/27-30

Listen to the poems and rhymes and read along.

1 **Pumpkin time at last**[1]

It's pumpkin time at last.
Let's play trick or treat.
It's pumpkin time at last.
And all our friends we'll meet.

Look at the costumes, everyone.
Ghosts and goblins[2], too.
Look at the costumes, everyone.
Now let's all shout "Boo!"

2 **It's time to fear**[3]**!**

The Halloween party is finally here.
You're not afraid? But it's time to fear!
For[4] ghosts and vampires[5] are very near.
Where do you want to hide, my dear?
The Halloween party is finally here.

3 **BOO!**

Here you are, dressed up alright[6].
You're looking great, hoping to fright[7].
But you see, I'm dressed up, too.
And I'll scare you when I go BOO!

4 **Mummies and monsters**

Mummies and monsters
Bats and rats[8]
Rats and cats
Cats and bats
Witches[9] wearing humpy[10] hats
Time for trick or treat

1 at last – endlich, **2 goblin** – Kobold, **3 time to fear** – Zeit zum Fürchten, **4 for** – denn, **5 vampire** – Vampir, **6 alright** – eindeutig, **7 hoping to fright** – in der Hoffnung zu erschrecken, **8 rat** – Ratte, **9 witch** – Hexe, **10 humpy** – bucklig

14b

Practise saying the poems and rhymes. Learn one of them by heart. Make a recording.

Challenge: Write your own Halloween poem or rhyme. You can rewrite one of the poems on this page.

LANGUAGE HELP Die einfache Gegenwart: Fragen TB S. 179

Bei Entscheidungsfragen im *simple present* stellst du *do* oder *does* an den Satzanfang.
Bei der 3. Person Singular verliert das Verb das -s am Ende. Beispiel: *Does Peter live in London? Yes, he does. / No, he doesn't.*

Bei Fragen mit Fragewort steht das Fragewort am Satzanfang. Beispiel: *Where does Peter live?*

Questions about festivals

15 CHOOSE YOUR LEVEL grammar: simple present TB p. 178, 180

I Read the answers. Then add the missing question words to the questions.

1 ______________ do you celebrate Christmas? – We celebrate on December 24th, on Christmas Eve.

2 ______________ does the Easter bunny live? – I don't know. Maybe each country has its own Easter bunny.

3 ______________ is going trick-or-treating with you? – My big sister and my little brother.

4 ______________ do you know when Chinese New Year happens? – It depends on the moon.

II Unscramble the questions.

1 the meaning · is · of Eid · What · ? ______________

2 festival · Is · a summer · Hanukkah · ? ______________

3 know · Halloween is · how old · Do you · ? ______________

4 What · about · Diwali · is · ? ______________

III Write questions for the answers.

1 ______________ ? – We look for Easter eggs in the garden.

2 ______________ ? – I like going to the Halloween parade.

3 ______________ ? – It is the festival of lights in India.

4 ______________ ? – I don't like it. It is silly to dress up and scare people.

Challenge: **Write answers to the questions in II.**

Spelling

16

Write the sentences in your exercise book. Which of the words start with a capital letter[1]?

1 MANY PEOPLE HIDE EGGS WHEN IT IS EASTER.

____

2 CHRISTMAS IS ALWAYS IN DECEMBER.

____

3 THE HOLI FESTIVAL IS A VERY COLOURFUL FESTIVAL IN INDIA.

____

4 THE CHINESE NEW YEAR CELEBRATIONS LAST THREE DAYS.

____

1 **capital letter** – Großbuchstabe

A festival poster TARGET TASK SUPPORT

17 wordbank: celebrations p. 163

1 Fill in the word web.

ideas for my festival poster

2 Collect words and phrases in the boxes.

When?	Where?
What is the background of this festival?	What do people do to celebrate?

3 Read the sentences for a gallery walk. What does the exhibitor[1] say? What does the visitor say? Write E for exhibitor, V for visitor or B for both[2] next to each sentence.

This is very interesting.	V
I think it's cool that …	
Thank you for your attention[3].	
My favourite thing about the festival is …	
Tell me more about … please.	
What is new for you?	
I didn't know anything about this festival.	
I like your poster because …	
Welcome. We are presenting …	
Can you tell me more about … ?	
Thank you for your presentation.	
Look at the poster. Do you have any questions?	
What do you find most interesting?	
What do you like about this festival?	

1 **exhibitor** – Aussteller/in, 2 **both** – beide, 3 **attention** – Aufmerksamkeit

Tipp: Höre dir vor eurem *gallery walk* die englischen Sätze an und sprich sie nach. audio 1/31

The bonfire party flyer

1

Write the correct phrases under the pictures.

see the spectacular fireworks · go for a ride at the funfair · get snacks from the food stalls · get a free face painting · watch the light show

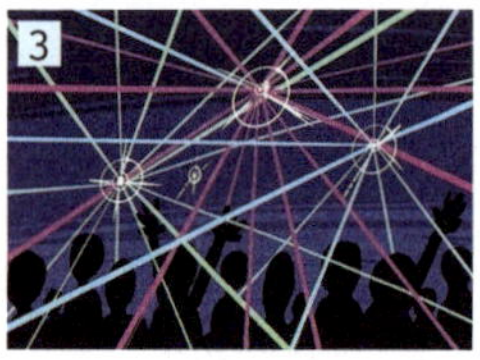

Would you go?

2 CHOOSE YOUR TASK

B: media worksheet 5, grammar: simple present TB p. 178-179, wordbank: celebrations TB p. 163

Would you like to go to a Bonfire Night party? Read the flyer in TB1b again.
Say what you think about the activities. You can use phrases or sentences from the switch board.

A **Make notes. Tell a partner.**
B **Make notes. Then make a recording and edit it.**
C **Write sentences in your exercise book.**

I like ...		I don't like ...
I don't like ...		I have to be at home by eight o'clock.
I really like ...	because	... sounds great.
I wouldn't go ...		I haven't got the money.
I think I would ...		I think it's not a good idea.
I would never ...		because I like to celebrate ...

Scrambled celebration words

3a

Unscramble the words and write them down.

ufniarf oskwreifr elvi scium rtcpasuceal nforbie ueuqe belrectea eotfef peslpa

3b

Think of more celebration words. Choose your favourite words and scramble them for a partner.

Unit 1A

Summer holidays (Seite 4)

1a: 1 was **2** were **3** was **4** were

1b: Beispiellösung:

In photo number 1 the boy is playing beach volleyball at the seaside. He is having fun.

In photo number 2 I can see water. People are at an adventure park.

In photo number 3 there is water, too. It is in Paris. I can see a sightseeing bus.

In photo number 4 there is a fantastic view of the mountains. The weather is nice. People are going hiking.

1c: Individuelle Lösung

Jason's summer holidays (Seite 4-5)

2 I: summer camp, north, outside, boys and girls, sunshine, brilliant, favourite, guitar

2 II: 1 false **2** false **3** true **4** false **5** false

2 III: 1 Jason's holiday was fantastic. **2** He went to a summer camp for boys and girls. **3** true **4** There was a campfire one evening. **5** There was a girl with a guitar.

Ava and Tarek's holidays (Seite 5)

3: Ava: + Ava was in Poland. She visited her grandma. She had a lazy horse. She had fun. She was happy. **-** Ava wasn't in London. She didn't stay at a hotel. She didn't go to a museum. She didn't play computer games. She wasn't sad.

Tarek: + Tarek was in Wales. He arrived on Friday. He milked a cow. He went cycling. He made fresh milkshakes. **-** Tarek wasn't in Italy. He didn't say that farms are boring. He wasn't afraid of cows. He wasn't in Wales with his uncle. He didn't feed the cows.

A farm holiday (Seite 5)

4: Tarek played with a cat. He didn't go for long walks. He learnt to bake bread. He didn't read a book. He didn't sit in the grass. He didn't feed the pigs. He wrote a diary.

Simple past (Seite 6)

5 stayed - stay, took - take, went - go, learnt - learn, loved - love, spent - spend, played - play , made - make, stood - stand, ate - eat, had - have, visited - visit

Karen's fantastic holidays (Seite 6)

6a I: had, was, had, went, loved, was

6a II: hiked, were, were, had

6a III: Beispiellösung:

Yesterday we went on a shopping trip to Vienna. Mum wanted to buy a new hat. Dad needed a souvenir for a friend. We had cake in a café. We liked it a lot. We also went to a museum. That was cool. We had a brilliant time. See you soon! Love, Karen

6b: 1 Where were they on holiday? **2** Did they like it? **3** How was the weather? **4** What did they do when they were hungry?

Practise reading: Back in Notting Hill (Seite 7)

7a: Individuelle Lösung

7b: Beispiellösung: **1** The picture shows a special old house in a forest. There is a street in front of the house. **2** The picture shows a street in a town. There is a castle in the background. **3** There is a sign with words in English and another language. You can see the sea in the background.

7c: Individuelle Lösung

Lily's new room (Seite 8)

8a-c: Individuelle Lösungen

Ellen's holiday (Seite 8)

9: Individuelle Lösung

Ava and her family (Seite 8)

10a: Individuelle Lösung

10b: /t/ milked, booked, laughed

/d/ moved, cycled, lived, happened
/id/ needed, waited, renovated, decided

Everybody's holiday (Seite 9)
11 I-III: Ava: Where: Poland **Who with:** --
What: visit grandma, went riding
Fun fact: had a lazy horse
Tarek: Where: Green Farm and Cardiff in Wales **Who with:** his dad **What:** milked a cow, the Welsh Folk Museum **Fun fact:** learned some Welsh words
Uncle Sami: Where: Italy **Who with:** --
What: stayed at a hotel, visited Rome
Fun fact: ate delicious Italian food
Ellen: Where: Spain **Who with:** her parents and her brother **What:** swam in the sea every day, went to a little town on a hill
Fun fact: bought a present for Ava

My amazing holiday (Seite 9)
12: busy, space, difficult, by the seaside, plane, unfortunately, strange, thousand, chickens, cows, tasted delicious, yesterday, tomorrow
Challenge: Individuelle Lösung

A holiday video (Seite 10)
13a: Maria, Lilly, Lewis
13b: Chloe went to Grimsby/stayed in a hotel near the beach/visited grandparents
Ben went to Spain/it was sunny and windy/ate lots of Spanish food/holiday was really nice
George went on holiday in the south of England/went camping/went on long walks

Rent a bike (Seite 10)
14 I-III: Beispiellösung:
1 Man kann einfach hingehen, aber sie empfehlen zu reservieren. **2** Die Preise kann man auf der Webseite nachsehen. **3** Man braucht einen Ausweis mit Bild (und Bargeld als Kaution). **4** Zwischen März und Oktober ist jeden Tag ab 9.30h geöffnet **5** Das hängt davon ab, wie beschäftigt sie sind.

My holiday post – Target task support (S.11)
15.1-2: Individuelle Lösungen
15.3: 1 Your blog post is really interesting/fascinating/brilliant/... **2** I liked the way you described your adventure holiday. **3** Could you please tell us more about ... **4** I think your blog post is a bit boring/too short/very complicated/... **5** You could write more about/add more ... to make it better. **6** Your blog post really makes me want to visit/to go to/find out more about ...! **7** I don't think that's a good idea.

Unit 1B
Talking about London (Seite 12)
1: Individuelle Lösung

More about the sights (Seite 12)
2: Individuelle Lösung

The most useful fact files (Seite 12-13)
3a: Individuelle Lösung
3b: Beispiellösung:
The London Eye is an expensive sight in London. The Tower of London is closer to a tube station than Buckingham Palace. The National History Museum is more popular than the Tower of London. Madame Tussauds is the most expensive sight. The Tower of London is a popular sight. The British Museum is more famous than the Science Museum. Madame Tussauds is more fun than the London Eye. The Tower of London is as close to a tube station as Madame Tussauds. The London Eye is the most interesting sight. The British Museum is more boring than Buckingham Palace.

Something else about London (Seite 13)
4a: C, B, E, A, D
4b I: the London Eye, Buckingham Palace, Hyde Park, Tower Bridge
4b II Beispiellösung:
the River Thames, the Houses of Parliament (the Palace of Westminster), (the Elisabeth Tower) Big Ben, St Paul's Cathedral, the Tower of London
4b III: sights that are on the map but not mentioned in the video: London Zoo, the Shard
London Zoo: London Zoo opened to the public in 1874. It is one of the oldest zoos in the world. You can see more than 19,000 animals and 673 different species there.
The Shard: The Shard is a very tall skyscraper in London. It was built in 2012 and is 309.6 metres high. It has 72 floors. From the top of the Shard you have a very good view.
Challenge: Individuelle Lösung

Tube announcements (Seite 14)
5: 2, 5, 1, 4, 3

Sights along ghe way (Seite 14)
6a: 3, 2, 7, 1, 5, 4, 6
6b: 1 to the river **2** Westminster Bridge **3** Big Ben **4** St James's park **5** Queen Victoria Memorial
6c: walk along 1x, walk on until 2x, turn right 2x, cross 2x, on your left 1x, go straight on 2x, walk past 1x, on your right 1x

Walk straight on (Seite 14)
7a+b: Individuelle Lösungen

Another sight(Seite 15)
8: 5, 9, 7, 1, 4, 3, 8, 6, 2

Sarah's favourite sights (Seite 15)
9 I: 1 Tower Bridge, the Museum of London, the Bank of England, Covent Garden, King's Cross Station
2 museums, King's Cross Station
9 II: 1 Sarah **2** Ellen **3** from a travel guide for kids **4** they want to do some shopping
9 III: 1 In the morning they want to go to Tower Bridge and the Tower of London. In the afternoon they plan to go to Covent Garden and King's Cross Station (platform 9 3/4).
2 They want to do some shopping and the shops there are lovely. **3** It's much too expensive. **4** It is famous from the Harry Potter films. In the film the children take the train to Hogwarts from there.
Challenge: Individuelle Lösung

Practise reading: Tower Bridge (Seite 16)
10a: a walk across a glass floor
10b: 1 inside Tower Bridge **2** every day from 9.30am to 6pm **3** It has a glass floor walkway. **4** 42 metres above the river and 33.5 metres above the road **5** £10.60 for adults and £5.30 for children **6** You can take the District and Circle lines to Tower Hill.

What's the best (Seite 17)
11: 1 the best, better, good **2** good, the best, better **3** good, better, the best

Sound check (Seite 17)
12a: Individuelle Lösung
12b: 1st syllable: parliament, yesterday, popular
2nd syllable: expensive, attraction, comparative, comparison
3rd syllable: entertainment, combination, exhibition
12c: Individuelle Lösung

A London quiz (Seite 17-18)
13a: 1 the home of the royal family
2 where you can find out about dinosaurs
3 a popular shopping area with street cafés
4 the name of a famous bell
5 a café and restaurant on a skyscraper
6 a ferris wheel with a great view of London
13b I-III: Individuelle Lösungen

A cable car ride (Seite 18)
14 I-III: 1 über die Themse **2** 34 **3** die Themse, die Skyline von London, Greenwich Peninsula, die Royal Docks und die O2 Arena **4** sechs Pfund **5** 5 bis 10 Minuten **6** zehn Menschen **7** in North Greenwich oder auf der Royal Victoria Seite des Flusses

Above the Thames (Seite 18)
15a-b: Individuelle Lösungen

A day out in London – Target task support (Seite 19)
16.1-3: Individuelle Lösungen

Unit 1 Check out (Seite 20-21)
1: 1 to Scotland **2** the Science Centre **3** for three days **4** to a village **5** It was sunny
2: 1 Arlo cycled with his friends on sunny days. **2** Lola visited her aunt in Spain for two weeks. **3** Tonya often helped her parents in their shop. **4** Abdul painted his room and read a lot of comics.
3: 1 Did you have fun in Wales? **2** How long did you stay there? **3** Did you go to the beach? **4** What else did you do in your holidays?
4: Beispiellösung:
Hyde Park is a large park in London. It has got many attractions. There is a large lake called the Serpentine. There are beautiful flower gardens and more than 3,000 trees. You can do many fun activities. For example, you can do sports like football, tennis or yoga, rent a boat or go to music events.
5: 1 Rabbits are small. Hamsters are smaller. Bees are the smallest. **2** Cows are tall. Horses are taller. Dinosaurs are the tallest.
3 Teenagers are young. Children are younger. Babies are the youngest. **4** Skateboards are expensive. Bikes are more expensive. Cars are the most expensive.
6: Beispiellösung:
Go straight on. Turn right onto Green Street and then left onto Penguin Road. Walk past the zoo. Walk on until you get to the Science Museum. Turn right onto Mill Road. Then turn left and cross Oxford Bridge. Turn left onto Park Street. On your right you can see Glenville Park. Then turn right onto Raven Road. Walk on until you get to the castle. It's on your right.

Unit 2A
Festival words (Seite 22)
1: Individuelle Lösung

More about the festivals (Seite 22)
2: 1 Hanukkah **2** Eid **3** Easter **4** Chinese New Year **5** Diwali
Challenge: Beispiellösung:
Hanukkah: celebrate in late November or December, nine candles, children get small presents each night

What people do to celebrate (Seite 22-23)
3 I: 1 On Christmas Eve **2** watches a play in church. **3** Grandpa **4** under the Christmas tree.
3 II: 1 People from India have the Holi Festival to celebrate the beginning of spring. **2** During the Holi Festval people are coloured in all the colours of the rainbow. **3** The Holi Festival usually takes place in March. **4** After the Holi Festival you can throw away your

clothes.
3 III: 1 The Day of the Dead takes place on October 31 every year. **2** It sounds scary, but it is a huge and cool festival. **3** People dress up as skeletons and paint their faces. **4** This festival is a bit like the American Halloween.

Celebration words (Seite 23)
4: traditional, believe, festival, celebrate, costume, religious, decorate, dancer
verbs: believe, celebrate, decorate
adjectives: traditional, religious
nouns: festival, costume, dancer

All over the world (Seite 23)
5: 1 in January or February, 15 **2** on different days, December 31 **3** Scotland, first
4 at twelve o'clock at night, twelve

Let's celebrate (Seite 24)
6a: Happy New Year
6b: Individuelle Lösung

Last New Year's Eve (Seite 24)
7a-c: Individuelle Lösungen

Sound check (Seite 24)
8a: Individuelle Lösung
8b: spring, religious, grape, lantern, dancer, fireworks, Easter, victory, really, information
8c: Individuelle Lösung

Chinese New Year (Seite 25)
9: Beispiellösung:
1 I saw an invitation for a Chinese New Year's celebration. **2** This year it is on January 31.
3 It starts in the morning. **4** with a special breakfast **5** After that the parents give money to the children. **6** In the evening there is a parade with music.
7 There is also a traditional dragon dance.
8 The dragon brings good luck to the people.
9 Then there is a big firework. **10** at 9 o'clock

Your Halloween word web (Seite 25)
10: Individuelle Lösung

Halloween tasks (Seite 25)
11.1: dragon
11.2+3: Individuelle Lösungen

Practise reading: Halloween today – opinions (Seite 26)
12a+b: Individuelle Lösungen

Your opinion (Seite 27)
13: Individuelle Lösung

Halloween poems and rhymes (Seite 27)
14a+b: Individuelle Lösungen
Challenge: Individuelle Lösung

Questions about festivals (Seite 28)
15 I: 1 When **2** Where **3** Who **4** How
15 II: 1 What is the meaning of Eid? **2** Is Hanukkah a summer festival? **3** Do you know how old Halloween is? **4** What is Diwali about?
15 III: Beispiellösung:
1 What do you do on Easter Sunday?
2 What do you do when it's Halloween?
3 What is Diwali? **4** What do you think about Halloween?
Challenge: 1 It is the end of Ramadan. **2** No, it is in winter. **3** It is about 2,000 years old.
4 It is about the victory of light over darkness.

Spelling (Seite 28)
16: 1 Many people hide eggs when it's Easter.
2 Christmas is always in December. **3** The Holi Festival is a very colourful festival in India. **4** The Chinese New Year celebrations last three days.

A festival poster - Target task support (S. 29)
17.1+2: Individuelle Lösungen
17.3: Beispiellösung:
Exhibitor: Thank you for your attention. My favorite thing about the festival is ... What is new for you? Welcome. We are presenting ... Look at the poster. Do you have any questions? What do you find most interesting? What do you like about this festival?
Visitor: This is very interesting. I think it's cool that ... Tell me more about ... please. I didn't know anything about this festival. I like your poster, because ... Can you tell me more about ...? Thank you for your presentation.
Both: My favorite thing about the festival is ... What do you find most interesting? What do you like about this festival? I think it's cool that ...

Unit 2B
The bonfire party flyer (Seite 30)
1: 1 get snacks from the food stalls
2 get a free face painting **3** watch the light show **4** see the spectacular fireworks
5 go for a ride at the funfair

Would you go? (Seite 30)
2/A-C: Individuelle Lösungen

Scrambled celebration words (Seite 30)
3a: funfair, fireworks, live music, spectacular, bonfire, queue, celebrate, toffee apples
3b: Individuelle Lösung

Sound check (Seite 31)
4a: Individuelle Lösung
4b: /ɒ/ bonfire, toffee, plot
/əʊ/ cold, bowl, almost
/ʌ/ love, cover
/ə/ forever, potato
/u:/ remove
/ɔ:/ northern, order
4c: Individuelle Lösung

Uncle Sami's plans (Seite 31)
5: Next Monday evening Uncle Sami is working late. Next Tuesday afternoon he is helping Tarek with his homework. Next Wednesday morning he isn't doing the shopping for the neighbours. Next Thursday evening he is going to dance class with Jennifer. Next Friday evening he isn't cooking dinner for the family. Next Saturday morning he is cleaning the house. Next Sunday he is going to an IT course.
Challenge: Beispiellösung:
The neighbours are going on holiday.
The family is going to a restaurant.

Getting ready for the bonfire party (Seite 32)
6a: 1 Ava's mum isn't decorating the house.
2 Ava's dad is bringing the wood for the fire.
3 Noah is writing invitations. **4** Ava is preparing toffee apples. **5** Sarah and Olivia aren't wearing their best clothes. **6** Harry is decorating the garden. **7** Joshua and Ava aren't making a salad. **8** Tarek's dad isn't buying fireworks.
6b: 1 Is Ava's mum decorating the house? No, she isn't. **2** Is Ava's dad bringing the wood for the fire? Yes, he is. **3** Is Noah writing invitations? Yes, he is. **4** Is Ava preparing toffee apples? Yes, she is. **5** Are Sarah and Olivia wearing their best clothes? No, they aren't. **6** Is Harry decorating the garden? Yes, he is. **7** Are Joshua and Ava making a salad? No, they aren't. **8** Is Tarek's dad buying fireworks? No. he isn't.

Getting ready for the party (Seite 32)
7 I: 1 some, any **2** some **3** some, any
7 II: 1 some, any **2** some **3** any **4** some
7 III: Individuelle Lösung

Practise reading: A recipe (Seite 33)
8a: Individuelle Lösung
8b: push into = Step 2, put into = Step 3, remove = Step 1, cover = Step 4, place in = Step 1, put on = Step 3, put in = Step 4, leave = Step 4

How to celebrate safely (Seite 34)
9: 1 simple safety rules **2** there are no animals **3** the sparkler, of cold water **4** stand far away **5** are still dangerous
Challenge: Individuelle Lösung

Sleeping hedgehogs (Seite 34)
10a: Individuelle Lösung
10b I-III: Beispiellösung:
bald ist Bonfire Night/das Poster gibt Sicherheitshinweise/bevor man ein Feuer macht, soll man das Wetter überprüfen und sich vor starkem Wind in Acht nehmen/unter dem Holz können schlafende Igel sein/kleine Kinder sollen nicht ans Feuer/nur Erwachsene dürfen Feuerwerk entzünden/man soll Feuerwerk nur im Freien entzünden, man soll Feuerwerkskörper nicht auf Menschen werfen oder in die Tasche stecken/man soll nicht versuchen Feuerwerkskörper zu entzünden, die man gefunden hat/Wunderkerzen sind nur für Kinder ab acht/sie werden mit ausgestrecktem Arm gehalten/man soll sie in einem Eimer Wasser löschen

Sound check (Seite 34)
11: man, hat, coffee, head, path, short, thing, read, bath, plane, gold, side

What Sarah says (Seite 35)
12 I: 1 message **2** before and after **3** save **4** very cool **5** fireworks
12 II: 1 a Bonfire Night party **2** made a plan **3** want to help, too **4** eat in the garden around the bonfire **5** They can have sparklers instead/watch the fireworks on TV.
12 III: Beispiellösung:
1 The children's plan is to have their own Bonfire Night party. **2** Ava and Noah are bringing wood and Ava is making toffee apples. **3** Olivia can decorate the garden. **4** Fireworks are expensive and bad for the environment. **5** They are going to celebrate and eat in the garden around the bonfire. Afterwards they are going to watch the fireworks display from Alexandra Palace in their living room.

A Bonfire Night picture (Seite 35)
13: Beispiellösung:
In the picture there is Harry and Lily, their mums, and Ava, Noah and Tarek. I can see the garden behind their house. The weather is cold but it isn't raining. Everybody is wearing warm clothes. There are two chairs. I can see many decorations in the garden. There is a box with more decorations and balloons. There is also a fire. They have got more wood next to the fire. I think they have got popcorn on the table. Lily is eating a toffee apple. Sarah and Olivia are sitting and having hot drinks. Harry and Lily are holding sparklers. Noah is roasting a marshmallow. Ava is holding her phone and a cup. I think she is writing a message. They seem to have a good time.

Pros and cons (Seite 35-36)
14a+b: Individuelle Lösung
Challenge: Individuelle Lösung
14c: 1 Mason **2** Willow **3** Stan **4** Grace **5** Amelia **6** Yussuf

Who is doing what? (Seite 36)
15 I: 1 The woman is taking a photo of the sparklers. **2** The boy is eating his food.

3 The women are singing a birthday song. **4** The man is bringing more food. **5** The cat is running away from the dog.
15 II: 1 No, she isn't. **2** Yes, they are. **3** No, it isn't. **4** Yes, she is. **5** No, they aren't.
15 III: 1 Who is smiling? **2** Who is running away from the dog? **3** Who is eating his food? **4** Who is singing a birthday song? **5** Who is bringing more food? **6** Who is taking a photo?

The party (Seite 36)
16: 1 many **2** many **3** a few **4** a little **5** much **6** a few 7 many

Our class party - Target task support (S. 37)
17.1+2: Individuelle Lösung
17 Tipp: Individuelle Lösung

Unit 2 Check out (Seite 38-39)
1: Diwali bells, oil for the lamps, candles, fireworks, food, new clothes
2: 1 false **2** true **3** false **4** true **5** false
3: Beispiellösung:
Hi, I'm Katy/Ben. We usually celebrate New Year's Eve at my aunt's house. We have a party with the whole family and some friends. We play fun games and dance to pop music. We have great party food and drinks. At midnight, we open the back door and let the old year out. We also sing a traditional song. Then we go outside, watch the fireworks and light sparklers. We always stay up very late.
4: 1 einen weißen Ballon, eine Schere, zwei weiße Plastiktüten, Klebeband, einen dicken schwarzen Filzstift **2** Man schneidet die Plastiktüten in lange dünne Streifen und klebt sie um den Ballon herum. Dann malt man die Augen und den Mund auf.
5: 1 on 12th April from 10am to 2pm **2** in the Central Gardens in Bridgewater **3** play games, ride ponies, listen to music, hunt eggs **4** It is free.
6: Next Saturday morning she is going shopping with her mum. Next Saturday evening she is watching a film with her family. Next Sunday morning she is meeting Ludo at the park. Next Sunday afternoon she is visiting her grandparents.

Unit 3A
Rules at your school (Seite 40)
1a-b: Individuelle Lösungen

More school rules (Seite 40-41)
2a: Beispiellösung: The students are not allowed to leave school at break and lunchtime. We can't wear make-up. They mustn't eat in class. You are allowed to drink in class. Boys have to wear their tie at all times. Girls' skirts mustn't be too short. You are not allowed to use your phone in lessons. You can only drink water in the classroom. You mustn't be late for your lessons. You have to be polite to others. They can't wear hats in the classroom. You must listen to your teacher. Boys can't have long hair. You mustn't bring your pet to school.
2b: A4, B5, C1, D3, E2

This is the headteacher speaking (Seite 41)
3 I: rules, uniform, lessons, teacher, polite, allowed
3 II: true: 1, 3
3 III: 1 general rules **2** bring heavy books **3** You can't use your phone **4** outside the classroom **5** politely **6** Because it is so hot

Sound check (Seite 41)
4: Beispiellösung:
There are different ways to pronounce the letter 'e'.

After school (Seite 42)
5a: 1H, 2E, 3G, 4A, 5D, 6I, 7C, 8B, 9F
5b: You hear sentences 1, 3, 5 and 9.

More school rules (Seite 42)
6/A-C: Individuelle Lösungen

School rules (Seite 42)
7: polite, respect, report, headteacher, office, correct, trouble, allowed, cap, break

Feelings (Seite 43)
8a: Beispiellösung:
1 good, happy, excited, relaxed **2** angry, annoyed **3** bored, tired **4** worried **5** scared
6 sad, terrible, unhappy
8b: Individuelle Lösung
8c I-III: Individuelle Lösungen

What they say (Seite 43)
9: Individuelle Lösung

Problems at home (Seite 44)
10a+b: Individuelle Lösungen

More problems (Seite 44)
11 I-III: Individuelle Lösungen

Practise reading: Ava'a diary (Seite 45)
12a: Individuelle Lösung
12b: Beispiellösung:
what Ava wants to do: wants to do what she wants, wants to wear her cool new jeans, wants to wear make-up, wants to use phone until ten, wants to come home later than seven, wants to listen to music and check her phone when she does homework
what Ava can't do or is not allowed to do: not allowed to wear cool new jeans for Dad's birthday party, not allowed to wear make-up, can't use phone up until ten, can't stay up late, can't be home later than seven, not allowed to listen to music or check phone when she does homework, can't play with Ollie before homework is finished

Mexidona's diary (Seite 46)
13: Beispiellösung:
das Trainingscamp: Er musste auch am Samstag früh aufstehen um ins Trainingslager zu fahren, aber er wäre viel lieber bei seiner Familie geblieben. Das Trainingslager war hart für ihn.
Regeln: Er durfte nicht essen was er wollte und nicht nach der Schule mit seinen Freunden spielen und musste früh ins Bett gehen. **Fotografen:** Er musste immer damit rechnen, dass vor der Haustür Fotografen auf ihn warteten. Darum musste er immer gut aussehen.

Your rules (Seite 46)
14: Individuelle Lösung

Am I allowed? (Seite 46)
15 I: 1 No, you can't. You must be home at nine. **2** No, you don't. I don't need help today. **3** Yes, you are. It's a good idea for the ummer months. **4** Yes, you may. It's delicious.
15 II: Beispiellösung
1 Yes, you are. But at home you have to drink water and tea. **2** Yes, you do. You're too young to stay out late. **3** Yes, you can. Take your football with you. **4** Yes, you may. But no more than ten people please.
15 III: Beispiellösung
1 May I go out shopping with my friends?
2 Can I wear make-up to the party?
3 Am I allowed to take another piece of cake?
4 Do I have to help you with dinner today?

A family meeting - Target task support (S. 47)
16.1-2: Individuelle Lösungen

Unit 3B

Flyers and pictures (Seite 48)
1: Individuelle Lösung

What is it? (Seite 48)
2: 1 squirrel **2** barbecue **3** nordic walking **4** horse riding **5** lead **6** camping **7** sun cream

More activities (Seite 48)
3/A: Individuelle Lösung
3/B: Beispiellösung:
The boy went to the National History Museum with his grandma and sister. He was in Southwold for a weekend with his mum and best friend. They visited his uncle. He went swimming and played beach volleyball. They ate chips and ice cream. Then he also was in New Forest National Park. The family went hiking.
3/C: Individuelle Lösung

Places in my area (Seite 48)
4: Individuelle Lösung

Dos and don'ts (Seite 49)
5a: 1 Don't touch the wild animals. **2** Take your rubbish away with you. **3** Don't feed the wild animals. **4** Respect other beach visitors. **5** Close gates behind you. **6** Don't swim in the sea when the flags are red.
5b I: 1 Don't swim **2** Swim **3** Don't touch **4** Take **5** Don't leave **6** Leave
5b II: Beispiellösung:
1 You must keep dogs on a lead. **2** You have to close gates behind you. **3** You are allowed to swim between the blue flags. **4** You mustn't touch the wild animals. **5** You can't play loud music. **6** You are allowed to camp on the campsites.
5b III: Beispiellösung:
Flyer 1: 1 Go to the website. **2** You are not allowed to feed the animals.
Flyer 2: 1 Don't swim in the sea when there is a red flag. **2** Don't use glass bottles.
Flyer 3: 1 Book a tour on the website. **2** You mustn't bring your dog without a lead.
Flyer 4: 1 You are not allowed to make a fire. **2** Close gates behind you.

A great day out (Seite 50)
6: 1 because I want to see wild animals. **2** because it is near Exeter. **3** although they must leave their dog at home. **4** because you can hire bikes at the information point.
Challenge: the connectives are: **1** because **2** because **3** although **4** because

In the forest on Sunday (Seite 50)
7 I: 1 at the wildlife centre last June. **2** at the beach last weekend. **3** in the forest on Sunday. **4** in New Forest National Park in the summer holidays. **5** in the forest in the afternoon.
7 II: 1 Alex and his friends went to Haldon Forest on Monday. **2** They ate cheese sandwiches at the Forest Café at luchtime. **3** Alex went horse riding in the park after the meal. **4** His friends took a bike tour through the park for an hour. **5** The boys came home late in the evening.
7 III: Beispiellösung:
My friend saw a fox in the forest on Sunday. We ate chips in a café last year. People found a phone on the street yesterday.
I had spaghetti in a restaurant on my holiday. My dad went fishing with a friend on the weekend.

Practise reading: A field trip (Seite 51)
8: a letter
The writer of the text: R. Patel
The writer's address: Holland Park School, Airlie Gardens, Campden Hill Rd, London W8 7AF

Who the text is written to: year 8 parents
8b: Where: to the British Wildlife Centre
When: on 25th March, 8am, 6pm
Who: students without payment and written permission
What: appropriate clothes, a packed luch and something to drink

What, when, why? (Seite 52)
9 I: 1 Where are the children? **2** What is Katy's job? 3 Are they starting with the bees?
9 II: 4 How can you help the hedgehogs?
5 Does the centre help the bees? **6** Where do hedgehogs sleep in the winter?
9 III: 7 What do you need a hammer for?
8 Why is it important to check the long grass?
9 Can you help the bees at home?
Challenge: Beispiellösung:
3 No, they are starting with the hedgehogs.
4 You can leave areas with long grass and dry leaves for them. **5** Yes it does: It builds "bee hotels" for them. **6** In a safe place. **7** To build a hedgehog house. **8** Because somethimes hedgehogs sleep there. **9** You can make a bee hotel in the garden or grow bee-friendly plants in flower pots.

Squirrels in the city (Seite 52)
10: Beispiellösung:
1 No, she has only seen red squirrels. She has never seen black or grey ones. **2** Yes, I think so. There is one squirrel that comes to her every day. **3** Yes, it does. It climbs up her leg. **4** Yes, she feeds it with nuts.
5 It likes unsalted peanuts. **6** She calls it Skippy. She thinks squirrels are very sweet and interesting.

An animal fact file (Seite 53)
11 I: Beispiellösung:
hedgehogs: a problem for hedgehogs: cars **what is difficult for them:** to find places to live and enough to eat **what they need in winter:** a safe place where they can sleep **what you can do to help them:** you can leave areas with long grass or dry leaves for them or build a hedgehog house **what you can feed them:** cat and dog food and water
11 II: Beispiellösung:
bees: what bees need to live: food, water and a place to live **where bees live at the centre:** in bee hotels **how many species produce honey:** only one in the UK **where bees live in nature:** some live in trees, some build nests in the ground **what you can do to help them:** build homes for them and grow lots of bee-friendly plants
11 III: Beispiellösung:
sea animals: sea animals that live in Britain: dolphins, porpoises, turtles and sharks
where you can see dolphins: Moray Firth, Scotland, in Wales, Cornwall
how do they live: in small groups of up to 15 animals
what sort of turtle can you see between May and September: leatherback turtles
how many kinds of sharks are there: 40

The children's project (Seite 53)
12a: 1 false **2** true **3** false **4** false **5** true **6** true
Challenge: Beispiellösung: **1** The reporter is in Notting Hill. **3** They are helping the bees. **4** They didn't have to ask anyone.
12b: Individuelle Lösung

More about the garden arts and crafts (Seite 54)
13 I: Beispiellösung. **1** You can make a hedgehog house. **2** In a quiet place in the garden. **3** You have to put some dry grass and leaves inside and cover it with earth.
13 II: Beispiellösung: **1** You can build an

insect hotel. **2** In a tree or on a wall. **3** You should fill the box with dry leaves and grass etc.
13 III: Beispiellösung:
1 You can make ice decorations with those things. **2** Outside or in a freezer if it's not cold enough outside. **3** You can hang it up in the garden or on the balcony.

Sound check (Seite 54)
14: You can hear five different pronunciations.
Our environment brochure - Target task support (Seite 55)
15.1-4: Individuelle Lösungen

Unit 3 Check out (Seite 56-57)
1: the school rules are: Students must not be late. Students must show respect to others. Students can't bring knives to school.
2: It's a good rule that we must be on time because that's also important for our future job. I think we should be allowed to use mobile phones because then we could search the Internet. In my opinion we should be allowed to drink water during lessons because it makes learning easier.
3: Beispiellösung:
Children younger than 12 years old are allowed to use the playground. Children under three are not allowed to come here alone. They can only play here when they come with an adult or children who are older than eight. Picnics and barbecues are not allowed.
4: The correct statements are: 4, 5
5: 1 true **2** false **3** false **4** true
6: 1 eight, thirteen **2** wildlife **3** environment, **4** plants, animals **5** wood, bird, hotels **6** Saturday

Unit 4A
Practise reading: A time capsule project (Seite 58)
1a: a container that you fill with objects of this time
1b: take part = teilnehmen, hand in = einreichen, a public opening = eine Öffnung vor Publikum
1c: Beispiellösung:
bring = bringen, project = Projekt, film = Film, museum = Museum, capsule = Kapsel, May = Mai

The children's future (Seite 59)
2a I: 1 A collage for her project. **2** There will be a public opening in 20 years. **3** Ava. **4** In a fancy flat in New York.
2a II: 1 You can hand in a drawing, a film, a poem or a story. **2** They will keep 15 works. **3** At the museum. **4** You leave your email address with them.
2a III: 1 What is the project about? **2** What does Ava think? **3** What is Tarek's plan? **4** Who will Harry bring to Tarek's restaurant?
2b: 1 drawing, film, poem **2** capsule, opening **3** chef, restaurant **4** hungry band, London **5** project **6** technology, food, houses **7** draw, future **8** record, guitar **9** Ava

Sound check (Seite 59)
3: Individuelle Lösung

The future for Erin, Mike and Lou (Seite 60)
4: Beispiellösung:
Picture 1: Maybe Erin will be a doctor. She won't get married and she won't have children. She will wear glasses. She will travel a lot.
Picture 2: I think Mike will be a chef. He will work in a nice restaurant together with two other people. He will have long hair. He will go hiking in the mountains. He won't have a TV and he won't have a car. He will get around on his bicycle.

Picture 3: Probably Lou will get married to a rich, good-looking man. They will have a lot of money and many children. They will also have a big car. Their house will be really nice and they will have a swimming pool.

A good job (Seite 60-61)
5a I-III: Individuelle Lösungen
5b: Beispiellösung:
1 police officer, firefighter **2** engineer, teacher, vet **3** pilot, gardener **4** baker, hairdresser **5** mechanic, hairdresser
6 fashion designer, photographer
Challenge: Individuelle Lösung

Four jobs (Seite 61)
6a: 1 police officer **2** chef **3** vet **4** actor
6b: chef, vet, police officer, actor

Prehaps you will be ... (Seite 61)
7a: Beispiellösung:
1 Maybe you'll be an actor/actress. **2** I think you'll be a vet/zoologist. **3** Perhaps you'll be a nurse/doctor. **4** Maybe you'll be a police officer. **5** I think you'll be a baker. **6** Perhaps you'll be a singer/rock star.
7b: Beispiellösung:
I like repairing bikes. Maybe I will be a bike mechanic. I like ...
Challenge: Beispiellösung:
My friend Frederic likes cooking. Perhaps he will be a chef. My cousin ...

Lots of jobs (Seite 62)
8/A: firefighter, mechanic, nurse, engineer, zoologist, hairdresser, teacher, pilot
8/B-C: Individuelle Lösungen

A job in Germany (Seite 62)
9 I-III: 1 The company SolarTech in Cologne (Köln) is looking for an engineer. They want the person to start as soon as possible.
2 They want someone to work in a team. The person should be friendly.
3 They are looking for someone who wants to learn about new technologies and who is not afraid of talking to customers. It's good to speak English.
4 They offer people who don't live in Germany a place to live. You can talk to them about the job online.
5 Send everything to the newspaper until 1st May.

Long and short (Seite 62)
10: it is - it's, you'll be - you will be, she is - she's, they have not - they haven't, he will not - he won't, I am - I'm, they don't - they do not, he'll - he will, she has got - she's got, they are - they're, she does not - she doesn't

Future questions (Seite 63)
11 I: Beispiellösung:
1 Will Ava stay in London? No, she won't.
2 Will Ava be a pilot? No, Joshua will be a pilot. **3** Will Ava need her skateboard? Yes, she will go to work on it. **4** Will Joshua be an engineer? No, he will be a pilot, a clown or a vet. **5** Will Joshua be a good vet? Yes, he will.
11 II: Beispiellösung: **1** Will Ava be a really cool engineer? Yes, she will. **2** Who will fly Ava to the USA or Germany? Joshua. **3** Will Joshua be a clown? Maybe. But perhaps he will be a pilot or a vet. **4** Who will take care of ill animals? Joshua. **5** Will Joshua have loads of pets? Yes, he will. He will have dogs and cats and maybe a panda.
11 III: Beispiellösung:
1 Will Ava invent things? Yes, she will. **2** Will Ava go to work by car? No, she won't. **3** What will Ava need to go to work? Her skateboard.
4 Who will definitely have children? Ava.
5 Will Joshua be a good vet? Yes, he will.
6 Why won't Ava have any pets? Because she

wants to travel a lot.

My future (Seite 63)
12: 1 what she wants **2** get a job in a café **3** By bus and she'll walk a lot. **4** She'll train to be a nurse.

A class survey (Seite 64)
13a I: Beispiellösung:
1 live **2** firefighter **3** be **4** design **5** work
13a II+III: Individuelle Lösungen
13b: Individuelle Lösung

Life in the future (Seite 64)
14a: Beispiellösung:
travel: no cars, solar-powered helicopters, bikes
learning: no exercise books, tablets
houses: smart home, VR glasses, bigger TVs
14b: Individuelle Lösung

In the future, there will be – a new verse (Seite 64)
15: Beispiellösung:
In the future there will be a lot of freedom, lot of freedom, lot of freedom, ...
In the future there will be a lot of children, lot of children, lot of children, ...

My ideas about the future - Target task support (Seite 65)
16.1-3: Individuelle Lösungen

Unit 4B
Who says it? (Seite 66)
1: 1 J, 2 J, 3 K, 4 J, 5 J, 6 J, 7 K, 8 J, 9 K

How do they talk? (Seite 66-67)
2a: Beispiellösung:
1 Kate: It looks like a tunnel. (slowly)
2 Jonathan: Watch out! (loudly)
3 Kate: Can't you walk faster? (angrily)
4 Kate: Yeah, yeah, I'm being careful. (calmly)
5 Jonathan: Oh. Spider. (worriedly)
6 Kate: I really wonder what we'll find. (excitedly)
7 Kate: Let me just see if... (nervously)
8 Jonathan: Kate? Where are you? (worriedly)
9 Jonathan: Look! It gives you the time, date and year. (proudly)
10 Kate: We could check out that dark corner at the back. (fast)
2b I-III: Beispiellösung:
1 In her room Kate speaks angrily. **2** In Kate's room Jonathan shouts loudly. **3** In the cellar Kate shouts excitedly. **4** In the cellar Jonathan talks fast. **5** On the stairs Kate whispers slowly. **6** In the cellar Jonathan asks worriedly. **7** In her room Kate answers proudly. **8** On the stairs Jonathan whispers nervously. **9** In her room Kate asks carefully.

How can you talk? (Seite 67)
3a+b: Individuelle Lösungen

What's the story like? (Seite 67)
4: Individuelle Lösung

Adverb wordsnake (Seite 68)
5: angrily, politely, quickly, nicely, badly, well, quietly, terribly, hard, dangerously

The adventure – part two (Seite 68)
6a: Individuelle Lösung
6b I: a slide, a tunnel
6b II: 1 Jonathan and Kate **2** Jonathan **3** Kate **4** Jonathan **5** Kate
6b III: 1 Jonathan calls Kate and then follows her into the tunnel. **2** Jonathan thinks it's scary. **3** Kate wants to go back to the house/ cellar. **4** He tells her to look at his watch. **5** He finds out that they are in the year 2128.
6c: Individuelle Lösung

Kate and Jonathan's adventure – part three (Seite 69)
7a: Individuelle Lösung
7b: beginning of 1st paragraph: The children were quiet for a moment.
beginning of 2nd paragraph: Their first idea was to walk back ...
beginning of 3rd paragraph: Then they tried to change the year ...
beginning of 4th paragraph: There it really became clear to them ...
Jonathan says: Oh dear. We really ARE in the future.
7c: 3, 4, 1, 2

Five questions (Seite 70)
8: Beispiellösung:
1 They try to go back into the tunnel and to change the year on Jonathan's watch.
2 She knows about Kate from the letter she found in the cellar. **3** Because it says in the letter that you can go back in time with the owner of the compass. **4** Georgia has virtual teachers, Jonathan and Kate have real teachers. Georgia uses solar-powered transport, Kate and Jonathan use the bus.
5 They have to write the letter and hide it in the cellar together with the compass so Georgia can find it in the future.

Practise your style (Seite 70)
9: 1 4, 8, 2, 5, 3, 9, 6, 7, 1
2 5, 3, 4, 1, 2

Double consonants (Seite 70)
10: carefully, disappear, tunnel, cellar, hill, compass, worried, brilliant, message, terribly, difficult, really

Imagine you had a time machine (Seite 71)
11 I-III: Beispiellösung:
Time they want to travel to:
Ella: the future in 300 years
Archie: to next Tuesday
Emily: in the past to the year 200
Ben: wants to stay in the present
Casey: to the future, just a hundred years
Place they want to travel to:
Ella, Archie, Emily: London
Ben, Casey: neighbourhood
Why?
Ella: She is curious, what will people invent?
Archie: Wants to take a look at his maths test.
Emily: See what London was like in the Roman times.
Ben: If you go to the past, you could change the present, if you travel to the future, you don't know where you'll end up.
Casey: See how people will live and what the neighbourhood will look like, will the school still be there?
Other information:
Ella: Bring some cool ideas back to the present.
Archie: Maybe he can get a good mark.
Emily: She saw an exhibition about Roman London.
Ben: It's really dangerous, has seen the film "Back to the future".
Casey: We already know a lot about the past, and we don't know anything about the future.

A report on science fiction (Seite 71)
12: Beispiellösung:
1 (Ein Fan ist, wer jedes Science Fiction Buch liest das neu rauskommt oder ins Kino geht wenn es einen neuen Science Fiction Film gibt.) Die folgende Information ist für Fans von Science Fiction interessant **2** In einem alten Haus in Brighton. **3** Eine berühmte Science Fiction Schriftstellerin. **4** Ein erstes Buch wird bald herauskommen und dann noch viele andere Bücher.

Sound check (Seite 71)
13a: Individuelle Lösung
13b: /ɑ:/ rather, calm, dark, paragraph
/æ/ thank, transport, camera
/e/ next, technology, ending, present

More on science fiction (Seite 71)
14/A-C: Individuelle Lösungen

Visitors from space (Seite 72)
15 I-III: Individuelle Lösungen
Challenge: Individuelle Lösung

My story - Target task support (Seite 73)
16.1-2: Individuelle Lösungen

Unit 4 Check out (Seite 74-75)
1: 1 It lasts five days. **2** You can build things and do experiments.
2: Beispiellösung:
Bella thinks that she will be a zoologist in Africa. She won't come home very often.
Eddie won't stay in London. He (thinks that he) will move to Wales and (he will) have a farm.
Lexi thinks that she will open her own baker's shop. She won't have more than two children.
3: 1 Liz is a nurse. She loves her job because she can take care of ill people. **2** Ron is a firefighter. He loves his job because he can help people in danger. **3** Fatma is a mechanic. She loves her job because she can learn new things all the time. **4** Patrick is a hairdresser. He loves his job because he can make people happy.
4: Beispiellösung:
1 surprised **2** terrible **3** worried **4** angry **5** excited
5: Logan ran to the bus stop quickly./Logan quickly ran to the bus stop.
Elsie can repair things easily./Elsie can easily repair things.
The Blunts left their old home sadly./The Blunts sadly left their old home.
The parents entered the baby's room quietly./The parents quietly entered the baby's room.
Please carry these new plates carefully./ Please carefully carry these new plates.
6: 1 When Rory woke up yesterday he felt very excited because it was his birthday.
2 He got up quickly and went to the living room, but no one was there. / He got up and quickly went ... **3** Rory got really sad, but suddenly the door opened and his family came in. **4** They gave him a white baby dog for a present so he was very happy for the rest of the day.

Unit 5A
Interesting places you know (Seite 76)
1: Individuelle Lösung

Discover the information (Seite 76)
2: The British Museum: mummy of a cat, Egyptian hieroglyphs
The Victoria and Albert Museum: modern trainers, glasses, old Egyptian shoes, theatre and musical costumes, hats
The Sherlock Holmes Museum: Dr Watson, violin, pipe collection, desk, microscope
Challenge: Beispiellösung: 2,000 pairs of shoes at the Victoria and Albert Museum/ the mummy of a cat at the British Museum is more than 4,000 years old/the Sherlock Holmes Museum is in a house from the 19th century/the Victoria and Albert Museum has 3,000 year old Egyptian shoes

Sherlock Holmes and Dr Watson (Seite 76-77)
3a: Beispiellösung:
Sherlock Holmes Museum house of the famous detective, his pipe collection, desk,

famous detective, his pipe collection, desk, violin and microscope are there, take picture of Sherlock Holmes, address is 221B Baker Street, Sherlock Holmes is character in a book

Challenge: Beispiellösung:
Dr Watson is the friend and assistant of Sherlock Holmes. He solves cases together with Sherlock Holmes. You can take a picture of him at the museum.

3b: Individuelle Lösung

What they have done (Seite 77)
4: Individuelle Lösung

Signal words (Seite 77)
5 I: 1 Ava has never seen a collection of old shoes before. **2** Harry has already read a story about Sherlock Holmes. **3** In the flyer they have put together lots of interesting information. **4** Tarek has actually seen a mummy before.

5 II: 1 The children have just looked at the museum flyer. **2** Harry hasn't seen the home of a detective yet. **3** Ava and Noah have been to five museums so far. **4** I have already checked my weather app ....

5 III: 1 Ava has never played the violin.
2 Lily and Harry haven't looked through a microscope yet. **3** Tarek has already read one of Sir Arthur Conan Doyle's books. **4** Lily has just found a flyer about museums.

Inside the museum (Seite 78)
6: I've read about that. They've put wax models all over the house. They've put that funny hat on his head. They've left a newspaper on his desk. They've put his violin next to his desk.

Let's go to the museum (Seite 78-79)
7 I-III: Beispiellösung:

1 Das Horniman Museum, Tate Modern und das Science Museum kann man kostenlos besuchen. Das London Transport Museum kostet nichts für alle unter 17.
2 Ins Horniman Museum.
3 Die Tate Modern ist eins der am meisten besuchten Museen in Großbritannien.
4 In die Tate Modern.
5 Auch in die Tate Modern.
6 Dann gehe am besten ins Science Museum.
7 Im London Transport Museum.
8 Das kannst du in der Tate Modern.
9 Das kann man im Horniman Museum, der Tate Modern und im Science Museum. Das kostet aber extra.

Lots of museums (S. 79)
8/A: Beispiellösung:
The Welsh Folk Museum (p.12):
open air museum, round house, old school house, hotel, old shops, farmhouses
The National History Museum (p.19):
history of life on earth, huge dinosaur exhibition **The London Transport Museum (p.25+108):** London's transport history, every type of vehicle that ever drove on London's streets **The British Museum (p.104):**
Egyptian hieroglyphs, mummy of a cat
The Victoria and Albert Museum (p.104):
more than 2,000 pairs of shoes, hats, glasses, costumes
The Sherlock Holmes Museum (p.104):
Sherlock Holmes's pipe collection, his desk, microscope, violin
The Science Museum (p.108):
science, technology, clocks, telescopes, telephones, planes, Apollo 10 space capsule
The Horniman Museum (p.108):
instruments, paintings, aquarium, stuffed walrus
The Museum of London (p.108):
history of London, Roman coins

Arsenal Football Club Museum (p. 109)
Wimbledon Windmill Museum (p. 109)
8/B-C: Individuelle Lösungen

Sound check (Seite 79)
9a-b: Individuelle Lösungen

A museum of everyday objects (Seite 79)
10: 1 It wasn't so boring.
2 Tarek thinks it's a nice idea to put normal things in a museum.
3 When Lily looks at her first lamp, she thinks of her time in Brighton.
4 The children want to have an exhibition for normal things that are special to them.

Lots of verbs (Seite 80)
11: regular verbs: use - used, play - played, smile- smiled, touch - touched, walk - walked, step - stepped, look - looked
irregular verbs: do - done, put - put, tell - told, see - seen, find - found, make - made, eat – eaten

What have you done? (Seite 80)
12a-b: Individuelle Lösungen
irregular verbs: do - done, put - put, tell - told, see - seen, find - found, make - made, eat – eaten

Practise reading: An exhibition of everyday things (Seite 81)
13a: Individuelle Lösung
13b: Beispiellösung:
1 vase colour 1: two painted roses, sculpted in 2022, 40 cm high, weighs 2.3kg
colour 2: Grandma Edyta, roses are her favourite flowers
2 lamp: colour 1: aluminum, plastic, 38cm high, weighs 1.3kg
colour 2: Lily designed it when she lived in Brighton, modern functional design
3 trainers: colour 1: pink, white stripes, size six, weigh 280g
colour 2: important role in Mrs Kogan's life, ran her first marathon in 2013
4 guitar: colour 1: wooden guitar for children, green, 62cm long, weighs 510g
colour 2: Harry's first guitar, played first tunes when he was five

At an exhibition of everyday life (Seite 82)
14a I: long brown hair, blue dress, pink lips, only one eye
14 II: Beispiellösung:
This very cool skateboard is 2 months old. It is red with yellow flames. The four wheels are yellow, too. It is very light and really great for practising tricks. (Stina practises the Ollie with it every day. It was a birthday present from her aunt and uncle.)
14 III: Individuelle Lösung (the object could be a ring with a blue stone)
14b: He is talking about the object on the right.

Sound check (Seite 82)
15a: You can hear five different pronunciations.
15b+c: ancient, newspaper, take

Our exhibition of everyday objects - Target task support (Seite 83)
16.1-2: Individuelle Lösungen

Unit 5B
Holiday activities (Seite 84)
1a: Individuelle Lösung
1b: Beispiellösung:
1 sounds really interesting. **2** because I like making things. **3** sounds terrible to me. **4** sounds a bit boring to me. **5** are not my thing. **6** creating things. **7** because I like ghost stories. **8** because I want to get better at playing football.
1c: Individuelle Lösung

What are they going to do? (Seite 84)
2 I-III: Beispiellösung: **1** Ava is going to go to Poland for two weeks. **2** Ava is going to visit her grandmother. **3** Tarek isn't going to go to the hockey camp. **4** He is going to do a drama workshop. **5** Lily is going to join the upcycling workshop. **6** Harry isn't going to act. **7** Lily and Ava are going to watch the performance. **8** At the drama workshop they are going to create a new version of the play. **9** Lily is going to create new things out of old stuff. **10** Tarek isn't going to do another cooking workshop. **11** Tarek is going to be on stage in a real theatre.

What is going to happen? (Seite 85)
3: 1 What **2** Where **3** When **4** Why **5** Who
Challenge: Beispiellösung:
1 old stuff (something she doesn't want or need anymore) **2** to her grandmother in Poland **3** the first two weeks of the summer holidays **4** Because he saw the note about the drama club on the noticeboard at the youth club **5** Harry.

Workshop words (Seite 85)
4: action, rubbish, course, art, youth, activity, drama, programme, coach, perform

Sound check (Seite 85)
5a: Individuelle Lösung
5b-c: /tʃ/ adventure, lunchtime, children, choose, China, picture, chain
/dʒ/ German, enjoy, jump, hedgehog, subject

A short version of the story (Seite 86)
6: 1 The Canterville Ghost lives in a very old house in the country.
2 One day, a family moves into the house: Mr and Mrs Otis and the twins, David and Jack.
3 The ghost wants them to move out again because it is his house.
4 So he tries to scare them away but no one in the family is afraid of him.
5 The ghost tries again and again and again and it's just not working.
6 He gets really angry and frustrated and tries all sorts of scary things.
7 But the family is just not scared of ghosts.

Something new for Harry (Seite 86)
7 I: 1 false **2** true **3** false **4** false **5** false
7 II: 1 true **2** true **3** false: the email address is right there on the website **4** false: Harry remembers Gus. **5** true
7 III: Beispiellösung:
1 false: Harry does not want to be on stage. He wants to do something with music or light. **2** false: You had to sign up by yesterday. / They are too late. **3** false: Gus is an American guy they know from a project at school. **4** false: The email address is on the website. **5** false: Gus teaches drama.
6 false: No, he doesn't feel motivated. / It's not working. / (At the end they are working.)

The drama workshop (S. 87)
8: 1 Is Harry going to act on stage? No, he isn't. **2** Is Harry going to do something with sound? Yes, he is. **3** Are Harry and Tarek going to look at the website? Yes, they are. **4** Is Harry going to laugh about the story? Yes, he is. **5** Is Harry going to do the guitar course? No, he isn't. **6** Is Harry going to write an email to Gus? Yes, he is. **7** Is Sir Simon going to scare the Otis family? No, he isn't. **8** Are Ava and Lily going to watch the performance? Yes, they are.

Gus' email to Harry (Seite 87)
9: 1 Tarek, drama project **2** write to me after the deadline **3** no places left **4** take her place now

At the start of the workshop (Seite 87-88)
10 I: 1 true **2** false **3** true **4** false
10 II: Beispiellösung:
1 would be good for him. **2** to put it on stage. **3** really liked it. **4** to need music for the play.
10 III: Beispiellösung:
Polly: really likes acting, read play at school, would like to put it on stage
Matt: is a bit shy, teacher said acting would be good
Harry: Tarek talked him into joining, he talked so much until Harry said yes
Tarek: really liked the drama project at school

Lots of ideas (Seite 88)
11: Individuelle Lösung

At the theatre (Seite 88)
12/A-C: Individuelle Lösungen

Practise reading: The Canterville Ghost (Seite 89)
13a-b: Individuelle Lösungen

How does the story end? (Seite 90)
14: Individuelle Lösung

After the performance (Seite 90)
15 I-III: Beispiellösung
1 Nein, sie spielen eine neue Version.
2 Es gibt sechs Schauspieler. **3** Die Rollen sind: die Zwillinge David und Jack, die Eltern (Mr und Mrs Otis), der Gespensterinspektor, das Gespenst Sir Simon. **4** Nein, das Stück ist lustig. **5** Ja, die Effekte für das Gespenst und das Rasseln der Ketten. **6** Das Publikum war begeistert. **7** Es wird bald eine weitere Vorstellung im Rainbow Theatre geben.
8 Sie dauert 1 Stunde und 35 Minuten und kostet £5. **9** Gus Graham.

Silly tongue twisters (Seite 90)
16a-b: Individuelle Lösung

Our play - Target task support (Seite 91)
17.1: Individuelle Lösung
17.2: 1, 3, 4

Check out 5 (Seite 92-93)
1: 1 have read **2** has never been **3** have just finished **4** has not/hasn't started yet
5 has travelled, has met
2: 1 Um 11:40 Uhr **2** Das Café
3 Um Besuchszeiten **4** In 15 Minuten
3: Lily has a large collection of socks. Some look really funny/cool. Lily's favourite socks are brown and look like rabbits. Her grandma gave them to her for her last birthday. As Lily loves science, she also has socks with different lab things on them. She often wears them to school. She has another cool / funny pair of socks which she only wears at home. She bought them when she moved to her new room. There is a text on them which says, "Don't talk to me. I'm reading".
4: 2 You don't have to pay for the meal.
4 You can play or produce music. **5** At the circus you can learn acrobat skills.
5: 1 Hamza is going to visit his aunt and uncle's family in Istanbul. **2** Willow and her brother Wayne are going to spend two weeks at a youth camp in Cornwall. **3** Finley is going to take part in a volleyball practice course at his sports club. **4** Binita is going to do a one-week bike tour with a group from her youth club.
6: Individuelle Lösung

Sound check

4a
audio 1/33

Learn to say the letter 'o'. Listen to the words and repeat them.

~~bonfire~~ · cold · toffee · northern · love · forever · plot · potato · cover · remove · order · bowl · almost

4b

Listen again and fill in the lists.

/ɒ/	/əʊ/	/ʌ/	/ə/	/uː/	/ɔː/
bonfire					

4c
audio 1/34

Listen again and check your lists.

LANGUAGE HELP Die Verlaufsform der Gegenwart: Aussagen mit Futurbedeutung

Du kannst mit dem *present progressive* ausdrücken, dass eine Handlung in der Zukunft liegt, indem du dem Satz eine Zeitangabe in der Zukunft hinzufügst. Beispiele: *Next Wednesday Tarek is playing hockey. He is meeting friends next Sunday.*

Uncle Sami's plans

5
grammar: present progressive TB p. 180

What is Uncle Sami planning for next week? Write sentences.

- *Monday evening: work late*
- *Tuesday afternoon: help Tarek with his homework*
- *Wednesday morning: ~~do the shopping for the neighbours~~*
- *Thursday evening: go to dance class with Jennifer*
- *Friday evening: ~~cook dinner for the family~~*
- *Saturday morning: clean the house*
- *Sunday: go to an IT course*

1 *Next Monday evening Uncle Sami is* ______
2 ______
3 *Next Wednesday morning he isn't* ______
4 ______
5 ______
6 ______
7 ______

Challenge: **Why have his plans for Wednesday and Friday changed? Think of reasons.**

Getting ready for the bonfire party

6a grammar: present progressive TB p. 180

Look at the pictures. What are the people doing? What are they not doing? Write in your exercise book.

bring the wood for the fire · decorate the house · write invitations · prepare toffee apples · wear their best clothes · decorate the garden · make a salad · buy fireworks

You can write: *Ava's mum isn't decorating the house.*

6b grammar: present progressive questions TB p. 181

Look at the pictures. Write yes / no questions and short answers in your exercise book.

You can write: *Is Ava's mum decorating the house? – No, she isn't.*

LANGUAGE HELP Die Mengenangaben some und any TB S. 182

Mit *some* und *any* bezeichnet man unbestimmte Mengen (z.B. 'einige', 'ein paar', 'etwas').
In Aussagesätzen benutzt man *some*. Beispiel: *We need some wood for the fire.*
In verneinten Aussagesätzen und den meisten Fragen benutzt man *any*. Beispiele: *There isn't any wood. Is there any tea?*

Getting ready for the party

7 CHOOSE YOUR LEVEL grammar: quantifiers TB p. 182

sparklers ✓
apple juice
marshmallows
music ✓
popcorn
apples ✓
wood
potatoes ✓

I Look at the list and complete the sentences. Use some or any.

1 The children have ________ apples, but they don't have ________ apple juice.

2 They need to get ________ marshmallows, too.

3 They already have ________ sparklers, so they don't have to buy ________ .

II Look at the list and complete the text. Use some or any.

1 The children have ________ apples for apple bobbing, but there isn't ________ apple juice to make hot drinks. 2 They have chosen ________ music for the party. 3 There aren't ________ marshmallows to make s'mores. 4 They also need to buy ________ popcorn.

III Look at the list. What do the children already have for the party? What don't they have? Write sentences. Use some or any.

Practise reading

Tipps 2 und Tipp 4
2 Wenn es zu einem Text Bilder gibt, sieh sie dir an. Sie können dir Hinweise auf den Inhalt geben.
4 Denke nach, bevor du liest! Oft ist es hilfreich, zu überlegen, was du schon über ein Thema weißt, bevor du einen Text darüber liest. Überlege auch, was du von einer bestimmten Textsorte weißt. Was erwartest du zum Beispiel in einem Rezept?

A Bonfire Night recipe

8a

Look at the pictures of this recipe. What can you see?

8b

A recipe tells you what you need to cook something and how to do it. Look at the list under "You need". Do you know all the words? Look up the words you don't know in the dictionary and write them down. What do you have to do? Look for the imperatives. Which step goes with the following imperatives?

push into *Step 2* put into ______ remove ______ cover ______

place in ______ put on ______ put in ______ leave ______

You need: 8 apples ______ 400 g sugar ______

1 tbsp lemon juice ______ 100 ml water ______

Step 1
Place the apples in a large bowl, then cover with boiling water.
Dry the apples and remove the stalks.

Step 2
Push a wooden skewer into each apple.

Step 3
Put the apples on a sheet of baking paper. Put the sugar and the water into a pot.
Cook for 5 minutes until the sugar melts, then add the lemon juice and boil a little longer.
You can test the toffee by putting a little into a bowl of cold water. It should get hard instantly.

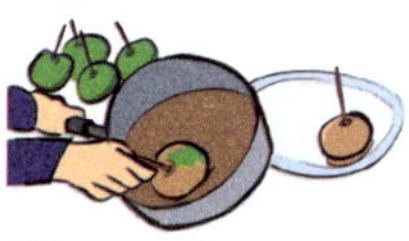

Step 4
Put each apple in the pot with the hot toffee and cover the apple with toffee,
then place it on the baking paper. Leave the toffee to cool before you eat your delicious toffee apples!

PRACTISE READING

Haben **Tipps 2 und 4** dir geholfen, den Text zu verstehen? ◯ ja ◯ teilweise ◯ nein

How to celebrate safely

9 video 5 media worksheet 1

Watch the video clip in TB8b again. Complete the sentences.

1 Then make sure to follow these ______________________ and enjoy the party.
2 Before you light your bonfire make sure that ______________________ hiding in the pile of wood.
3 When ______________ has finished, put it in a bucket ______________ .
4 As with sparklers ______________________ while you light them.
5 Fireworks that haven't gone off ______________________ .

Challenge: Which of the tips do you find most important? Why? Write about your opinion.

Sleeping hedgehogs

10a skill: reading TB p. 154

Read the poster. What is it about? Take notes on the information.

10b CHOOSE YOUR LEVEL skill: mediation TB p. 155

Explain the poster to a friend in German.
Tell your friend

- I **four facts or more.**
- II **six facts or more.**
- III **eight facts or more.**

Sound check

11 audio 1/39

Read the pairs of words. Then listen and repeat. Underline the words you hear.

man · men had · hat toffee · coffee head · had path · pass sort · short
sing · thing read · lead path · bath plan · plane gold · cold sight · side

What Sarah says

12 CHOOSE YOUR LEVEL audio 1/38, skill: listening TB p. 151

I Listen to TB9 again. Underline the correct words.

1 Sarah read Harry's letter / message / notes on the way home.

2 For party at home you have to do a lot of work before / after / before and after the party.

3 A party at home means they can earn / bring /save some money.

4 Olivia always has crazy / very cool / the best ideas for decorating the garden.

5 She doesn't like fireworks / sparklers / bonfires.

II Complete the sentences.

1 Harry wants to organize

2 The friends already

3 All the other parents

4 They can celebrate and

5 They can't have fireworks but

III Answer the questions in your exercise book.

1 What is the children's plan?
2 What is Ava and Noah's job?
3 What can Olivia do?
4 Why are fireworks a bad idea?
5 What are they going to do at the party?

A Bonfire Night picture

13 media worksheet 5

Look at the picture in TB 12b again. Who is in it? What is happening? What are they doing? Make notes first. Then talk for one minute or longer. Make a recording and edit it.

You can say:
In the picture there are …
I can see …
The weather is …
There are many …
There is also …
They have got …
I think they …
… is eating …
… are having …
… are holding …
… is roasting …
They seem to …

Pros and cons

14a

Read the pros and cons[1] for Bonfire Night parties. Underline them in green (pro) and red (con). Then sort the arguments. Start with 1 for the argument that is most important for you.

☐ fireworks are fun to watch
☐ some parties are expensive
☐ there are too many people
☐ it's very loud
☐ you can play party games
☐ a party with friends is fun
☐ fireworks are bad for the environment
☐ rides on a funfair are great

1 **the pros and cons** – das Für und Wider

14b

Compare your pros and cons from 14a with a partner. Where do you agree? Where do you disagree?

Challenge: **Think of more arguments. Write them down and sort them as in 14a.**

14c audio 1/41

Listen to the children. What do they think about bonfire parties? Match the statements and the names.

1 Bonfire Night parties without fireworks are less fun.
2 Having a good time together is the most important thing.
3 At big organized parties there is something to do for everyone.
4 Having a party with friends is better than big organized parties.
5 Bonfire Night parties are bad for animals.
6 Watching fireworks displays is safer and more spectacular.

Amelia	
Stan	
Yussuf	
Mason	
Willow	
Grace	

Who is doing what?

15 CHOOSE YOUR LEVEL grammar: present progressive TB p.180

Look at the picture on p. 31 of your textbook. Write in your exercise book.

I What are the people doing? Write sentences.

The woman The boy The women The man The cat	is are	taking singing eating running bringing	more food. away from the dog. a photo of the sparklers. his food. a birthday song.

II Do exercise I. Then answer the questions.

1 Is the woman dancing?
2 Are the women singing a birthday song?
3 Is the dog running away from the cat?
4 Is the woman taking a photo?
5 Are the children eating ice cream?

III Who is doing what? Do exercise I. Then write questions to the anwers.

1 The grandfather.
2 The cat.
3 The boy.
4 The women.
5 The man.
6 The woman.

LANGUAGE HELP Die Mengenangaben much, many, (a) little und (a) few TB S. 182

much (viel) benutzt man vor nicht zählbaren Nomen im Singular. Beispiel: *much water*
many (viele) benutzt man vor zählbaren Nomen im Plural. Beispiel: *many bottles*

little (wenig) und *(a) little* (ein wenig) benutzt man vor nicht zählbaren Nomen im Singular. Beispiel: *a little water*
few (wenige) und *(a) few* (einige) benutzt man vor zählbaren Nomen im Plural. Beispiel: *a few bottles*

The party

16 grammar: quantifiers TB p. 182

Read the sentences and underline the correct words.

1 There are much / many people at the party. 2 We have much / many great songs on our playlist.
3 Only a little / a few people are dancing to the music. 4 There is a little / a few time left before the party is over.
5 How much / many food is still on the table? 6 There are a little / a few snacks.
7 We have much / many bottles of lemonade left.

Our class party TARGET TASK SUPPORT

17 wordbank: celebrations TB p. 163

1 Think of different kinds of parties and what is special about them. Fill in the table.

What kind of party?	Why is it fun?	What would we need?

2 Collect ideas for the party you want to organize. Think of …

games and activities

decorations

our class party

food and drinks

more ideas

Tipp: Nehmt euch genügend Zeit für die Vor- und Nachbereitung
Nehmt euch genügend Zeit für die Vorbereitung eurer Party und überlegt euch auch genau, was ihr danach aufräumen müsst und wer dafür verantwortlich ist. Denn nach der Party muss alles bald wieder tadellos aussehen. Dann dürft ihr bestimmt auch bald wieder eure nächste Klassenparty planen.
Schreibt alle Aufgaben auf, die wichtig sind. Unterscheidet sie in **vor, während** und **nach der Party**.
Was müsst ihr als Klasse tun? Wofür bist du verantwortlich? Schreibe es dir auf.

Vor der Party muss ich ____________________

Während der Party ist es meine Aufgabe, ____________________

Nach der Party werde ich ____________________

Die Check out-Seiten helfen dir einzuschätzen, was du schon gut kannst und was du noch üben solltest. Löse die Aufgaben auf dieser Doppelseite und male die Kreise wie auf Seite 20 rot, gelb oder grün aus.

1 Kannst du ein Telefongespräch über Pläne für ein Fest verstehen?
2 Kannst du kurze Texte zu Feiertagen und Festen verstehen?
3 Kannst du erzählen, was du üblicherweise an einem Feiertag oder Fest machst?
4 Kannst du Bastelanleitungen auf Deutsch wiedergeben?
5 Kannst du einen Flyer zu einer Veranstaltung verstehen?
6 Kannst du darüber schreiben, was jemand für die nähere Zukunft plant?

1 audio 1/42

Listen to Madura and her mother. What do they still need for Diwali? Tick the right answers.

☐ flowers → ☐ Diwali bells → ☐ new lamps
☐ oil for the lamps → ☐ candles → ☐ fireworks
☐ food → ☐ new clothes → ☐ presents

Ich kann ein Telefongespräch über Pläne für ein Fest verstehen. ○

2

Read about Passover. Then tick ✓ true or false.

Passover is the most important Jewish festival. It is at the end of March or in April and it lasts for about a week. I really enjoy it because the whole family gets together. On the first and second night of Passover we have a special meal called a Seder. Before we start eating, we read prayers and sing songs. Traditionally, the youngest child asks four questions about why the Seder night is different from other nights. The celebrations are good fun, but they usually last so long that I sometimes fall asleep at the table.

	true	false
1 Passover is in summer.	☐	☐
2 It lasts for about seven days.	☐	☐
3 A Seder is a Passover prayer.	☐	☐
4 The family has a Seder on two nights.	☐	☐
5 The oldest child asks four questions about the Seder.	☐	☐

1 Passover – Passahfest

Ich kann kurze Texte zu Feiertagen und Festen verstehen. ○

3

You are Katy or Ben. Talk about your celebrations on New Year's Eve. Make a recording.

* usually celebrate at aunt's house
* party: whole family, some friends
* fun games, dance to pop music
* great party food and drinks
* midnight: open back door, let old year out
* also sing traditional song
* go outside, watch fireworks, light sparklers
* always stay up very late

You can say:
Hi, I'm Katy / Ben.
We usually celebrate New Year's Eve …

Ich kann erzählen, was ich üblicherweise an einem Feiertag oder Fest mache. ○

4

Find out how to make another Halloween decoration. Then answer the questions in German.

Balloon ghost
A balloon ghost is a great Halloween decoration and it is really easy to make. You need a white balloon, a pair of scissors, two white plastic bags, some tape and a thick black felt-tip. Cut the plastic bags into long thin pieces. Use the tape to put them around the balloon. Draw two eyes and a mouth on the balloon. This ghost looks scary and it flies really well!

1 Welche Materialien braucht man?

2 Wie geht man vor?

Ich kann Bastelanleitungen auf Deutsch wiedergeben.

5

Read the flyer and answer the questions.

Free Easter Egg Hunt
Easter Sunday, 12th April
10:00am to 2:00pm
Hunt at 12:00pm
GAMES • PONY RIDES • MUSIC
Central Gardens | Bridgewater

1 When is the Easter egg hunt?
2 Where is it?
3 What can you do?
4 How much does it cost?

Ich kann einen Flyer zu einer Veranstaltung verstehen.

6 grammar: the present progressive TB p. 180

What is Arla doing next Saturday and Sunday? Write about her plans.

Saturday:
* morning: go shopping with mum
* evening: watch film with family

Sunday:
* morning: meet Ludo at park
* afternoon: visit grandparents

Next

Ich kann darüber schreiben, was jemand für die nähere Zukunft plant.

Wenn du noch mehr üben möchtest, gehe zu Practise more – Unit 2. DIGITAL+

Rules at your school

1a grammar: simple present questions TB p. 179

What are the rules at your school? Answer the questions with short answers from the box.

No, we can't. · Yes, we do. · No, we aren't. · Yes, we can. · Yes, we are. · No, we don't.

1 Can you do your homework at school? ____________
2 Are you allowed to eat during lessons? ____________
3 Do you have to be polite to the teachers? ____________
4 Are you allowed to be late? ____________
5 Can you wear a hat or cap during lessons? ____________
6 Are you allowed to speak German in your English lesson? ____________
7 Do you have to clean up the classroom after lessons? ____________

1b wordbank: rules TB p. 164

Read TB1b again. Talk about your school rules.

You can say:

At our school we …
Our teachers always say that …
They tell us to …
Rule number … is different.
We don't have rule number …
Our school …
Here students are allowed to …
We can't …

More school rules

2a CHOOSE YOUR LEVEL grammar: modal verbs TB p. 183-184

Write about school rules. There are many different possibilities.
Write … I five or more sentences II seven or more sentences III ten or more sentences.

The students	are not allowed to	wear	make-up.
We	can't	shout	in class.
They	mustn't	eat	your pet to school.
You	are allowed to	drink	their tie at all times.
Boys	have to	be	too short.
Girls' skirts	can only	use	your phone in lessons.
…	must	leave school	late for your lessons.
	…	listen to	at break and lunchtime.
		bring	polite to others.
		have	hats in the classroom.
		…	water in the classroom.
			your teacher.
			long hair.

LANGUAGE HELP Das Modalverb needn't TB S. 183

Mit *needn't* (Kurzform von *need not*) kannst du ausdrücken, dass etwas nicht notwendig ist.
Beispiel: *Yesterday, Ava tidied her room. Today she needn't tidy it again.*

2b

Match the sentence parts.

A In German schools
B You tidied your room yesterday,
C Mum already made dinner,
D The cage is nice and clean,
E There is a lot of food in the fridge,

1 so Dad needn't do it today.
2 so we needn't buy any today.
3 so we needn't clean it today.
4 students needn't wear a tie to school.
5 so today you needn't tidy it again.

A	
B	
C	
D	
E	

This is the headteacher speaking

3 CHOOSE YOUR LEVEL audio 2/1

I Listen and tick ✓ the words you hear.

☐ rules → ☐ exercise → ☐ uniform

☐ lessons → ☐ teacher → ☐ pencil

☐ polite → ☐ allowed → ☐ drinking

II Listen. Are the sentences true or false? Tick ✓.

	true	false
1 You needn't bring heavy books.	☐	☐
2 You can use your phone in class.	☐	☐
3 You must wait quietly outside.	☐	☐
4 You have to keep to the right.	☐	☐
5 You can run and shout in the hall.	☐	☐

III Listen and tick ✓ the correct sentence endings.

1 The headteacher starts with	☐ important rules.	☐ general rules.	☐ the correct rules.
2 You needn't	☐ wear the uniform.	☐ bring heavy books.	☐ bring other school things.
3 Especially during lessons	☐ you can use your phone.	☐ you have to listen.	☐ you can't use your phone.
4 Before lessons you must wait	☐ outside the classroom.	☐ quietly inside.	☐ in the school grounds.
5 You have to talk to others	☐ in a friendly way.	☐ nicely.	☐ politely.
6 You are allowed to drink	☐ all the time.	☐ because it is so hot.	☐ tea and lemonade.

Sound check

4 audio 2/3

Learn to say the letter 'e'. Listen to the words and repeat them. What do you notice?

get · respect · dangerous · television · her · helmet · report · we · English · were · be

After school

5a

Look at the picture.
What do you think the children are thinking or saying?
Match the sentence parts.

1 Our school uniform
2 I'm happy
3 It's so hot today
4 We have
5 Let's
6 Today is such
7 I'm looking forward to
8 I had a great
9 Why do we even have to

A so much homework.
B day at school today.
C seeing Ollie.
D meet in the park later.
E school is over for today.
F wear blazers in the middle of summer?
G and I just want to relax a bit.
H is so horrible.
I a hot day.

1	H	
2		
3		
4		
5		
6		
7		
8		
9		

5b audio 2/4

Listen to Ava, Tarek and Lily in TB6b again. Tick ✓ the four sentences you hear.

More school rules

6 CHOOSE YOUR TASK wordbank: rules TB p. 164

A **Write some rules for teachers.**
B **Talk to a classmate. What do they think about school rules? Make notes.**
C **Design a school uniform. Present it to the class.**

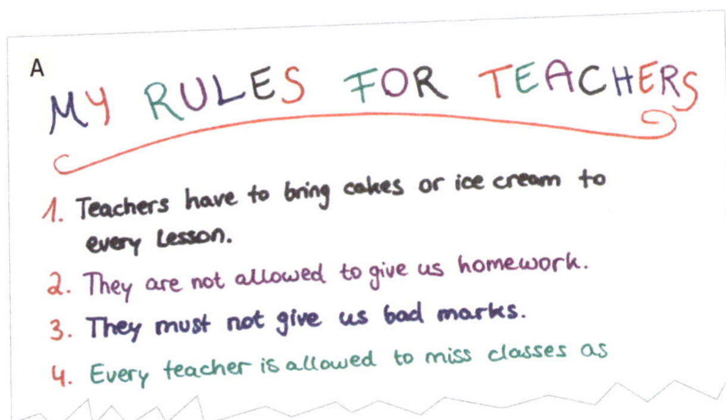

School rules

7

Find the words in the word snake.

Feelings

8a

wordbank: talking about conflicts TB p. 165

Look at the faces. How does the girl feel? Use adjectives from the box.

good · happy · sad · bored · tired · worried · scared · angry · annoyed · relaxed · terrible · unhappy[1] · excited[2] · ...

1 **unhappy** – unglücklich, 2 **excited** – aufgeregt, begeistert

1 

4 

2 

5 

3 

6 

8b

Compare your ideas with a partner's ideas.

8c

CHOOSE YOUR LEVEL wordbank: talking about conflicts TB p. 165

When do you feel happy, scared, angry, ...?
Write about ...
I two feelings. II three feelings. III five feelings.

You can write:
I feel ... when ...
I feel ... after ...
Sometimes I am ... because ...

What they say

9

wordbank: talking about conflicts TB p. 165

Write down what Ava and her family say or think.

2

3

1

5

4

Problems at home

10a

media worksheet 5, wordbank: talking about conflicts TB p. 165

Choose one of the scenes from TB7a and talk about it. Make a recording. Edit your recording.

You can say:

Picture A: Tarek is in his room reading a comic. His room is very messy. His things are everywhere. His ... and ... are on the floor. On his desk ... On his chair ... Next to him on his bed there is ... His dad comes in and says ...

10b

wordbank: talking about conflicts TB p. 165

Choose one of the scenes from TB7a. Imagine it is one week later. Write about what is happening.

A Tarek is in his room. His dad comes in.
B Harry and Lily are sitting at the dinner table with their mums.
C Noah comes home from playing football with his friends in the evening.
D Ava and her family want to go out to a friend's birthday party.

You can write:

It is one week later. Tarek is in his room again reading a book. ... Suddenly, someone knocks on the door. His dad comes in and ...

More problems

11

CHOOSE YOUR LEVEL wordbank: talking about conflicts TB p. 165

I Look at the picture. What do you think Tarek and his dad are thinking or saying? Write down your ideas in your exercise book.

Tarek: You're late. I'm hungry.

Dad: I forgot to get the pizza.

II Look at the picture. What do you think Noah and his mum are thinking or saying? Write a dialogue in your exercise book.

Mum: What have you done to your hair?

Noah: I like it that way.

III Look at the picture. What do you think Ava, Joshua and their mum are saying? Write a dialogue in which they find a solution to the problem.

Joshua: I found them. They are all alone.

Mum: We can't keep them.

Ava: But they are so cute.

Practise reading

Tipps 1 und 5

1 Bevor du einen Text liest, sieh dir die Überschrift an und überlege, worum es gehen könnte.
5 Während du liest, kann es dir helfen, Informationen in einem Text zu unterstreichen oder zu markieren. Dann kannst du sie in einer Tabelle, einem Diagramm oder einem Wortnetz ordnen.

Ava's diary

12a

Read the title. What is a diary? What do you write in a diary? Make notes.

12b

Read the diary entry. Find information about the topics in the table. Underline it and fill in the table.

Wednesday, 7th February

Why can't I do what I want? Mum always knows better.

I've got some cool new jeans but Mum says I'm not allowed to wear them to Dad's birthday party. And I'm not allowed to wear make-up.

Everybody else can use their phone until ten. I can't. Mum says I must be in bed by half past nine. Rules, rules, rules! That's all we have in this house! I hate them!!!

And I always have to be home by seven. Then there is homework! I'm not allowed to listen to music or check my phone while I'm doing it. And I have to finish it before I can go out or play with Ollie.

On Saturday we are having a family meeting to discuss when Noah and I have to be at home at the weekend.

I hope Dad is on our side. Sometimes he's not as strict as Mum.

what Ava wants to do	
what Ava can't do or is not allowed to do	

PRACTISE READING

Haben **Tipps 1 und 5** dir geholfen, den Text zu verstehen? ○ ja ○ teilweise ○ nein

Mexidona's diary

13 skill: mediation TB p. 155

Du bist mit deiner kleinen Schwester in London im Fußballmuseum. Sie ist ein Fan des berühmten Fußballers Mexidona und versteht den Tagebucheintrag nicht. Erzähle ihr, was Mexidona als Kind geschrieben hat über
· das Trainingscamp · die Regeln · die Fotografen.

23rd March 1998
Last Saturday I had to get up at five o'clock and get ready for training camp. The bus left at six. Why do I always have to go away from my family? I miss them so much. I want to sleep late and have a nice family breakfast. Training at the camp is so hard.
I'm not allowed to eat what I want so that I don't get fat. I can't play with my friends after school because I have to go to training every day. I must be in bed at nine o'clock so that I get enough sleep. RULES! RULES! RULES! I hate them! I can't even wear what I want. I always have to look good when I leave the house because often there are photographers waiting for me. Sometimes I must answer silly questions for a newspaper. I always have to be polite and smile and mustn't show my feelings or say what I think. Why can't I be a normal boy?

Your rules

14 grammar: modal verbs TB p. 183-184

Write rules for your bedroom door. Complete the sentences or write your own rules.

You can write:
You are not allowed to … Mums and dads must … I can get up when … You mustn't take … Don't knock on the door before … o'clock.

Am I allowed?

15 CHOOSE YOUR LEVEL grammar: modal verbs TB p. 183-184

I Match / the questions and answers. Write them in your exercise book.

1 Can I go out until ten o'clock tonight? — Yes, you are. It's a good idea for the summer months.
2 Do I have to help in the kitchen? — Yes, you may. It is delicious.
3 Am I allowed to cut my hair very short? — No, you don't. I don't need help today.
4 May I give you another piece of cake? — No, you can't. You must be home at nine.

II Write answers to the questions.

1 Am I allowed to drink lemonade at the party? ______
2 Do I have to be home at eight o'clock? ______
3 Can we play in the park until dinner time? ______
4 May I invite all my friends to my birthday party? ______

III Write questions to the answers.

1 ______ Yes, you may. But you have to be home on time.
2 ______ No, you can't. You're too young to wear make-up.
3 ______ Yes, you are. Give me another piece, too, please.
4 ______ Yes, you do. I need your help today.

A family meeting TARGET TASK SUPPORT

16 wordbank: talking about conflicts TB p. 165, skill: performing a scene TB p.159

1 Write down: the reason for the conflict, the rules the family has, the pros and cons. Also write down who takes part in the family meeting. Who plays which role?

Reason for the conflict / Rules

Pros	Cons

Who takes part? Who plays the role?

2 Complete the sentences. Then choose the sentences you want to use in your role play.

Welcome to today's family meeting.

Our first point is: ______

Why can't I ______ ?

Why do I have to ______ ?

Don't interrupt ______

We think that you're still too young to ______

I don't think ______

I don't like it when you ______

We said that you ______

It is not fair when you say ______

All my friends can ______

It wasn't my mistake, I ______

Maybe we could try to ______

What about trying it for ______ ?

Tipp: Beherzige diese Regeln für ein gutes Gespräch:

1. Jeder kann ein Anliegen vorbringen.
2. Jede Meinung ist gleich viel wert.
3. Alle hören einander zu.
4. Alle sind freundlich und höflich zueinander.
5. Niemand wird unterbrochen.
6. Die getroffene Entscheidung soll eine gute Entscheidung für alle sein.

Flyers and pictures

1

Look at the pictures in TB1a. Describe what you see.

beach · pier · people playing ball · the sea · fox · people in swimming costumes · bicycle · forest · deer · sandcastle · horses · helmet · ponies · surfboard

You can say:
I see …
On flyer number 1 I see a …
In picture 2 there is …
On the right of picture 2 I see …

What is it?

2

Find the answers in TB1.

1 A small, grey or red, animal that climbs trees: ____________

2 You are not allowed to do this at Southwold Beach: ____________

3 You need long poles[1] for this activity: ____________

4 A sport you need an animal for: ____________

5 It is helpful to walk your dog: ____________

6 When you do this, you sleep in a tent: ____________

7 You put it on when you go in the sun: ____________

1 **poles** – Stöcke

More activities

3 CHOOSE YOUR TASK

B: audio 2/7

A **What are your most difficult words in TB1?**
Choose 5-10 words.
Practise spelling them.
Then write sentences with them.
You can write: *barbecue – We made a fire in the garden and had a barbecue.*

B **Listen to the boy.**
Which of the places in TB1 did he go to?
Who did he go with?
What did he do there?
Take notes.

C **Imagine you went to one of the places in TB1.**
What was it like? Write about it.

Places in my area

4

Write about interesting places in your area and what you can do there.

You can write:
In my area there is …
The … is close to our town.
My friend sometimes goes to …
At home, we have a flyer about …
I know about a place called …
There you can …
We always go there to …
It is a place where you can …

1 DIE EINFACHE VERGANGENHEIT: BEJAHTE AUSSAGEN

the simple past: positive statements TB p.174

Wenn du über etwas sprechen willst, das in der Vergangenheit liegt und abgeschlossen ist, verwendest du die einfache Vergangenheit *(simple past)*. Es gibt regelmäßige und unregelmäßige Verben.

Das *simple past* der regelmäßigen Verben bildest du, indem du die Endung -ed an die Grundform anhängst. Die Formen sind bei allen Personen gleich: *stay + ed → stayed* *look + ed → looked* *visit + ed → visited*

Die unregelmäßigen Verben haben im *simple past* eine eigene Form, die du lernen musst: *have → had* *go → went* *do → did*

Das Verb *be* hat als einziges Verb zwei Formen im *simple past*, *was* und *were*: *I / he / she / it was – you / we / they were*

Eine Liste mit unregelmäßigen Verben findest du im TB auf S. 247-248.

2 DIE EINFACHE VERGANGENHEIT: VERNEINTE AUSSAGEN

the simple past: negative statements TB p.175

Wenn du sagen willst, was in der Vergangenheit nicht passiert ist, benutzt du bei den meisten Verben *didn't (=did not)*. *Didn't* ist die Vergangenheitsform von *don't* und *doesn't* und bei allen Personen gleich. Es folgt das Verb in der Grundform.

Bejahte Aussage	Verneinte Aussage
I went to Paris last year.	I didn't go to London last year.
Ava talked to Lily yesterday.	Ava didn't talk to Tarek yesterday.

Bei *was* und *were* hängst du nur *not* oder die Kurzform *n't* an, wenn du einen verneinten Satz bilden willst.

Bejahte Aussage	Verneinte Aussage
I was in London last year.	I wasn't in Paris last week.
They were friendly at the hotel.	They weren't friendly at the restaurant.

3 DIE EINFACHE VERGANGENHEIT: FRAGEN

the simple past: questions TB p.176

Bei Entscheidungsfragen im *simple past* stellst du *did* an den Satzanfang. *Did* ist bei allen Personen gleich. Danach folgt das Verb in der Grundform. In der Kurzantwort wird *did* wieder aufgegriffen.

Entscheidungsfrage	Kurzantwort	Kurzantwort
Did you go on holiday?	Yes, I did.	No, I didn't.
Did Harry visit his grandparents?	Yes, he did.	No, he didn't.

Bei Fragen mit *was* und *were* brauchst du kein *did*. Hier steht *was* oder *were* am Satzanfang. In der Kurzantwort wird *was* oder *were* wieder aufgegriffen: *Was the weather good?* *Yes, it was./No, it wasn't.*

Bei Fragen mit Fragewort steht das Fragewort am Satzanfang: *What did you do in the holidays?* *Where did you go?*

Wenn *who* nach dem Subjekt fragt, brauchst du kein zusätzliches *did*: *Who went to Poland?*

Auch bei Fragen mit *was* und *were* brauchst du kein *did*: *How was your holiday?* *What were your favourite places?*

4 DIE STEIGERUNG VON ADJEKTIVEN

the comparison of adjectives TB p.177

Möchtest du Personen oder Dinge vergleichen, kannst du Adjektive steigern.

Einsilbige und einige zweisilbige Adjektive werden durch das Anhängen von *-er* und *-est* gesteigert:
Tower Bridge is tall,
Big Ben is taller,
but the London Eye is the tallest.

Mehrsilbige Adjektive werden mit *more* und *most* gesteigert:
London Zoo is popular,
the Natural History Museum is more popular,
but Buckingham Palace is the most popular sight.

Bei manchen Adjektiven ändert sich die Schreibweise (z.B. big – *bigger*, *easy – easier*, *nice – nicer)* und einige haben unregelmäßige Formen, die du lernen musst wie Vokabeln, z.B.: *good – better – (the) best* *bad – worse – (the) worst*.

In Vergleichssätzen benutzt du den Komparativ mit *than*: *Noah is older than Ava.*
Sind die Eigenschaften gleich, benutzt du *as ... as*: *Lily is as old as Harry.*

5 DIE EINFACHE GEGENWART: AUSSAGEN *(REVISION)*

the simple present: statements (revision) TB p. 178

Die Zeitform *simple present* benutzt du, wenn jemand etwas regelmäßig tut, wenn etwas regelmäßig stattfindet oder wenn etwas über längere Zeit oder allgemein gültig ist. *Das simple present* hat meistens die gleiche Form wie die Grundform des Verbs: *I love Christmas.* *We always celebrate it with the family.*
In der 3. Person Singular *(he, she, it)* hängst du ein -s an: *My little brother loves Christmas, too.*

Für die Verneinung fügst du in den meisten Fällen *don't (= do not)* bzw. *doesn't (=does not)* ein:
I don't celebrate Christmas. *The Chinese New Year doesn't take place on the same day every year.*

6 DIE EINFACHE GEGENWART: FRAGEN *(REVISION)*

the simple present: questions (revision) TB p. 179

Wenn du im *simple present* Entscheidungsfragen stellen möchtest, musst du in den meisten Fällen *do* oder *does* an den Satzanfang stellen. In den Kurzantworten wird *do* oder *does* aufgegriffen.

Entscheidungsfrage	Kurzantwort	Kurzantwort
Do you celebrate Eid?	Yes, I do.	No, I don't.
Does your sister like her presents?	Yes, she does.	No, she doesn't.

Bei Fragen mit dem Verb *be* steht kein *do* oder *does* am Satzanfang. Statt dessen benutzt man die entsprechende Form von *be*, also *am, are* oder *is*: *Are you from London? – Yes, I am. / No, I'm not.*
Bei Fragen mit Fragewort steht dieses am Satzanfang vor *do* oder *does*: *What do you know about Eid? When does it start?*
Wenn man nach dem Subjekt fragt, braucht man bei Fragen mit *who* kein *do* oder *does*: *Who likes presents? Who gets socks?*

7 DIE VERLAUFSFORM DER GEGENWART: AUSSAGEN *(REVISION)*

the present progressive: statements (revision) TB p. 180

Das *present progressive* verwendest du, um zu beschreiben, was gerade passiert. Du kannst es aber auch verwenden, um über Pläne für die (nähere) Zukunft zu sprechen. Du bildest es mit einer Form von *be* + Grundform des Verbs + Endung *-ing*.
Achte auf die Schreibweise. Endet das Verb auf ein stummes *-e*, dann fällt das *-e* in der *ing*-Form weg:
have → having – I am having a party. dance → dancing – Everybody is dancing.

Endet das Verb auf einem kurzen betonten Vokal + Konsonant, wird der Konsonant verdoppelt:
put → putting – Tarek is putting food on the table. run → running – Ava is running.

Für die Verneinung fügst du *not* hinter der Form von *be* ein. Hier wird dann häufig die Kurzform verwendet:
I'm not making pizza. Harry isn't dancing.

8 DIE VERLAUFSFORM DER GEGENWART: FRAGEN *(REVISION)*

the present progressive: questions (revision) TB p. 181

Mit dem *present progressive* kannst du fragen, was jemand gerade tut oder was jemand für die (nähere) Zukunft plant. Entscheidungsfragen bildest du, indem du die Form von *be* an den Satzanfang stellst. In den Kurzantworten wird die Form von *be* aufgegriffen.

Entscheidungsfrage	Kurzantwort	Kurzantwort
Are you going home next weekend?	Yes, I am.	No, I'm not.
Is your brother coming?	Yes, he is.	No, he isn't.
Are your friends staying at home?	Yes, they are.	No, they aren't.

Bei Fragen mit Fragewort steht dieses am Satzanfang: *What are you doing next week? When is your friend coming over?*

9 MENGENANGABEN

quantifiers TB p. 182

Mengenangaben wie *some* und *any* verwendest du, wenn du keine genaue Menge oder Anzahl von etwas nennen möchtest. Auf Deutsch bedeuten *some* und *any* so viel wie „einige", „ein paar" oder „etwas".
In bejahten Aussagesätzen verwendest du *some*: *There are some apples in the kitchen. I need some milk for my cornflakes.*
In verneinten Aussagesätzen und bei den meisten Fragen verwendest du *any*: *There isn't any milk. Are there any apples?*

Auch *much, many* und *a lot of* sind Mengenangaben, die man vor allem in Fragen und verneinten Aussagesätzen verwendet.
Much (auf Deutsch „viel") wird mit Nomen verwendet, die nicht zählbar sind: *We haven't got much milk.*
Many (auf Deutsch „viele") wird mit Nomen verwendet, die zählbar sind: *How many apples have we got?*

In bejahten Aussagesätzen verwendet man eher *a lot of* oder *lots of*. Hier braucht man nicht zwischen zählbaren und nicht zählbaren Nomen zu unterscheiden: *We need lots of juice and lots of snacks for the party.*

10 DIE MODALVERBEN *MUST* UND *MUSTN'T*

the modal verbs must and mustn't TB p. 183

Die Wörter *must* und *must not (mustn't)* benutzt du z. B., wenn du über Regeln sprechen willst.

Mit *must* kannst du sagen, was jemand tun muss. *Must* steht mit der Grundform des Hauptverbs zusammen und ist in allen Personen gleich: *Students must wear the correct school uniform. Harry must wear a tie.*

In der Regel kannst du *must* durch *have to* oder *has to* ersetzen:
Students have to wear the correct school uniform. Harry has to wear a tie.

Must hat keine eigene Vergangenheitsform. Daher wird die *simple past*-Form von *have to* benutzt:
Yesterday, Ava had to tidy her room.

Wenn du sagen willst, was jemand nicht tun muss, benutzt du *don't have to* bzw. *doesn't have to:*
Today, Ava doesn't have to tidy her room.

Mit *mustn't* kannst du sagen, was jemand nicht tun darf. Es steht mit der Grundform des Hauptverbs zusammen und ist in allen Personen gleich: *Ava mustn't listen to music when she does her homework. Students must not run in the school building.*

11 DIE MODALVERBEN *CAN, BE ALLOWED TO* UND *MAY*

the modal verbs can, be allowed to and may TB p. 184

Die Wörter *can, be allowed to* und *may* benutzt du um auszudrücken, dass etwas erlaubt oder nicht erlaubt ist.

Can bedeutet können, aber auch dürfen. *Can* steht mit der Grundform des Hauptverbs und ist in allen Personen gleich:
We can bring our mobiles to school, but we can't use them during lessons.
Mit *can* kannst du auch um Erlaubnis fragen: *Dad, can I go out and play football? – Yes, you can, but only for an hour.*

Auch *be allowed to* heißt dürfen. Die Form von *be* musst du an die Person anpassen. Für die Verneinung fügst du *not* hinzu:
I'm allowed to stay out until eight o'clock. My little brother is not allowed to watch TV after seven o'clock.
Fragen mit *be allowed to* stellst du so: *Are you allowed to bring your mobiles to school? What are you allowed to do?*

Mit *may* und *may not* drückst du aus, was jemand tun darf bzw. nicht tun darf. Die Form ist bei allen Personen gleich und steht mit der Grundform des Verbs: *You may use your mobiles at break. You may not use them during lessons.*
Mit *may* kannst du auch höflich um Erlaubnis fragen: *May I open the window, please?*

12 DIE WORTSTELLUNG IM AUSSAGESATZ *(REVISION)*

word order in statements (revision) TB p. 185

Aussagesätze werden nach einem bestimmten Muster gebildet: Subjekt – Verb – Objekt (S – V – O). Danach können noch Ergänzungen wie z. B. Orts- oder Zeitangaben folgen. Werden Ort und Zeit genannt, steht zuerst der Ort.

Subjekt	Verb	Objekt	Ortsangabe	Zeitangabe
Harry	loves	cooking.		
He	cooks		in the school kitchen	every Tuesday.
Ava	sees	her friends	at school	every day.

Die Reihenfolge S – V – O gilt auch für Nebensätze: *Tarek goes to the cooking club because he loves cooking.*

Beachte auch die Position von Häufigkeitsadverbien wie *always, usually, often, sometimes* oder *never*.
Das Häufigkeitsadverb steht fast immer vor dem Verb: *We often play football in the park.*
Das Häufigkeitsadverb steht hinter der Form von *be*: *My friend is often late.*

13 DAS FUTUR MIT *WILL*: AUSSAGEN

the will-future: statements TB p. 186

Wenn du über die Zukunft sprechen möchtest, kannst du das *will-future* verwenden. Damit kannst du auch Vermutungen anstellen oder Vorhersagen machen. Es wird mit *will* und der Grundform des Verbs gebildet. Die Form *will* ist bei allen Personen gleich.
Beim Sprechen verwendet man meist die Kurzform *'ll*, beim Schreiben meist die Langform.
Für die Verneinung fügst du *not* hinter *will* ein = *will not*. Die Kurzform ist *won't*.

Langform	Kurzform	Langform	Kurzform
I will be famous.	I'll be famous.	We will live in London.	We'll live in London.
I will not have a regular job.	I won't have a regular job.	They will not have cars.	They won't have cars.

14 DAS FUTUR MIT *WILL*: FRAGEN

the will-future: questions TB p.187

Bei Entscheidungsfragen im *will-future* steht *will* am Satzanfang. Du verwendest *will* bzw. *won't* auch in den Kurzantworten:

Entscheidungsfrage	Kurzantwort	Kurzantwort
Will I be a famous fashion designer?	Yes, you will.	No, you won't.
Will you live in New York?	Yes, I will.	No, I won't.
Will Harry be rich?	Yes, he will.	No, he won't.

Bei Fragen mit Fragewort steht das Fragewort am Satzanfang: *Where will you live?* *What will Lily's job be?*

15 ADVERBIEN DER ART UND WEISE

adverbs of manner TB p. 188

Wenn du beschreiben möchtest, wie jemand etwas tut oder wie etwas geschieht, benutzt du Adverbien der Art und Weise.

Ein Adverb bildest du, indem du an das Adjektiv die Endung *-ly* anhängst:

Adjektiv	Adverb
loud	loudly
bad	badly
slow	slowly

Manchmal ändert sich die Schreibweise, wenn *-ly* angehängt wird:

Adjektiv	Adverb
easy	easily
terrible	terribly
beautiful	beautifully
fantastic	fantastically

Einige Adverbien haben Sonderformen, die du wie Vokabeln lernen musst. Manche Adjektive und Adverbien sind gleich:

Adjektiv	Adverb
good	well
fast	fast
hard	hard

16 VERBINDUNG VON SÄTZEN MIT *LINKING WORDS*

linking words TB p. 189

Linking words sind Verbindungswörter, mit denen du Sätze oder Satzteile miteinander verbinden kannst.
Die Konjunktionen *and, or* und *but* z. B. verbinden Hauptsätze miteinander:

1. Hauptsatz		**2. Hauptsatz**
Jonathan's new watch had a bright torch,	and	it could also tell the time, date and year.
The children had to find a way back,	or	they would have to stay in the future.
They tried to change the year on the watch,	but	the watch simply changed it back to 2128.

Andere Konjunktionen verbinden einen Haupt- und einen Nebensatz, z. B. *because* und *when*.

Hauptsatz		**Nebensatz**
The children hid in the bushes	because	they wanted to see who lived in the house.
They were surprised	when	they saw Georgia.

17 DAS PERFEKT: AUSSAGEN

the present perfect: statements TB p. 190

Das *present perfect* verwendest du, wenn etwas irgendwann in einem Zeitraum von der Vergangenheit bis zur Gegenwart passiert ist sowie wenn ein Vorgang in der Vergangenheit noch Auswirkungen auf die Gegenwart hat. Du bildest es mit *have / has* + Partizip Perfekt *(past participle)* oder den ensprechenden Kurzformen. Bei regelmäßigen Verben bildest du das Partizip Perfekt, indem du an die Grundform des Verbs die Endung *-ed* anhängst:
I have cleaned the kitchen. I've done the shopping. He has finished his homework. He's tidied his room.
Die Formen der unregelmäßigen Verben musst du auswendig lernen wie Vokabeln:
I have been to the British Museum. Lily has found a flyer. We have read a story.

Die Verneinung bildest du mit *haven't / hasn't* + Partizip Perfekt: *I haven't cleaned the kitchen yet. He hasn't had lunch yet.*

18 DAS PERFEKT: FRAGEN

the present perfect: questions TB p. 191

Mit einer Entscheidungsfrage im *present perfect* kannst du z. B. nachfragen, ob jemand etwas in der Vergangenheit schon einmal gemacht hat. Du bildest sie, indem du *have* oder *has* an den Satzanfang stellst.

Entscheidungsfrage	**Kurzantwort**	**Kurzantwort**
Have you ever been to London?	Yes, I have.	No, I haven't.
Has Ava bought a new book?	Yes, she has.	No, she hasn't.

Bei Fragen mit Fragewort steht das Fragewort am Satzanfang: *What have you done? Where have you been?*

Bei Fragen und Aussagen werden häufig Adverbien der unbestimmten Zeit verwendet, z. B. *ever* (= jemals), *never* (= nie), *already* (= schon), *just* (= gerade) und *not yet* (= noch nicht). Die meisten Adverbien stehen direkt vor dem Partizip Perfekt:
Have you ever been to London? – No, I've never been there.
Has Ava already taken Ollie for a walk? – Yes, she has just come back.
Beachte die Ausnahme: *yet* steht am Satzende: *Have you ever been to London Zoo? – No, I haven't been there yet.*

19 DAS FUTUR MIT GOING TO: AUSSAGEN

the going to-future: statements TB p. 192

Wenn du über Pläne für die Zukunft sprechen willst, kannst du das *going to-future* verwenden. Man verwendet es auch bei Ereignissen, die wahrscheinlich eintreten werden. Im Deutschen gibt es keine entsprechende Zeitform.
Du bildest das Futur mit *going to* mit einer Form von *be* + *going to* + Grundform des Verbs.
Für die Verneinung stellst du *not* hinter die Form von *be*. Auch hier wird häufig die Kurzform verwendet.

Langform	**Kurzform**	**Langform**	**Kurzform**
I am going to do a workshop.	I'm going to do a workshop.	We are going to act in a play.	We're going to act in a play.
I am not going to leave.	I'm not going to leave.	Harry is not going to act.	Harry isn't going to act.

20 DAS FUTUR MIT GOING TO: FRAGEN

the going to-future: questions TB p. 193

Mit einer Frage im *going to-future* kannst du z. B. danach fragen, was jemand für die nächsten Ferien plant.
Bei Entscheidungsfragen rückt im *going to-future* die Form von *be (am, is, are)* an den Satzanfang. In der Kurzantwort steht dann die entsprechende Form von *be*.

Entscheidungsfrage	**Kurzantwort**	**Kurzantwort**
Are you going to do a cooking workshop?	Yes, I am.	No, I'm not.
Is Ava going to visit her grandmother?	Yes, she is.	No, she isn't.
Are the children going to act in a play?	Yes, they are.	No, they aren't.

Bei Fragen mit Fragewort steht das Fragewort an erster Stelle:
What are you going to do in the holidays? When is the workshop going to start? Where is it going to be?

Dos and Don'ts

5a

Look at TB1 again. Read flyers 2 and 4. Match ⁄ the sentence parts.

1 Don't touch	in the sea when the flags are red.
2 Take	the wild animals.
3 Don't feed	other beach visitors.
4 Respect	the wild animals.
5 Close	your rubbish away with you.
6 Don't swim	gates behind you.

5b CHOOSE YOUR LEVEL grammar: modal verbs TB p. 183-184

I Read flyers 2 and 4 again. Complete the dos and don'ts.

1 ______ when the flags are red.

2 ______ between the blue flags.

3 ______ the wild animals.

4 ______ nothing but photographs.

5 ______ your rubbish behind.

6 ______ nothing but footprints.

II Read flyers 1, 2 and 4 again. Complete the dos and don'ts.

1 You must ______

2 You have to ______

3 You are allowed to ______

4 You mustn't ______

5 You can't ______

6 You ______

III Read the flyers again.
Write two sentences about each flyer in your exercise book.
Use words from the boxes.

must · can · don't · be allowed to · mustn't · ...

feed · swim · watch · take · go · keep · touch · book · close · leave · get · use · find · watch · ...

You can write:
Go to ...
You are not allowed to ...

LANGUAGE HELP Die Wortstellung im Nebensatz TB S. 185

Nach dem Hauptsatz können noch weitere Ergänzungen folgen. Dann steht auch der Nebensatz in der Reihenfolge Subjekt – Verb – Objekt (S – V – O). Beispiel: *Tarek goes to the cooking club because he loves cooking.*
Die Angabe des Ortes steht vor der Angabe der Zeit. Beispiel: *He plays in the park every day.*

A great day out

6 grammar: word order TB p. 185

Unscramble the second half of the sentences. Write down the whole sentence.

1 I'd like to go to the British Wildlife Centre, want to see / I / because / wild animals

2 You can get to Haldon Forest easily by car, is / because / near Exeter / it

3 My friends often go to Southwold beach, at home / must leave / they / their dog / although

4 You don't need to bring your own bike, you can hire / because / at the information point / bikes

Challenge: Underline the connective in each sentence.

In the forest on Sunday

7 grammar: word order TB p. 185

I Put the sentence parts in brackets into the correct position. Write down whole sentences.

1 Alex saw a fox. (at the wildlife centre / last June)
2 Jacob went swimming. (last weekend / at the beach)
3 We took a Nordic walking tour. (in the forest / on Sunday)
4 Katie went camping. (in the summer holidays / in New Forest National Park)
5 Emily and Emma went to the café. (in the forest / in the afternoon)

II Unscramble the sentences and write them down.

1 Alex – on Monday – to Haldon Forest – and his friends – went
2 cheese sandwiches – at lunchtime – they – ate – at the Forest Café
3 after the meal – in the park – Alex – horse riding – went
4 for an hour – a bike tour – his friends – took – through the park
5 home – late in the evening – came – the boys

III Write five sentences or more about a day out.

My friend We People I My dad ...	had saw ate found ...	chips fishing spaghetti a fox ...	on the street in a restaurant with a friend in the forest ...	on my holiday. last year. on the weekend. ...

Practise reading

Tipps 4 und 10

4 Denk nach, bevor du liest! Oft ist es hilfreich, zu überlegen, was du über ein Thema weißt, bevor du einen Text liest. Überlege auch, was du über eine bestimmte Textsorte schon weißt – was erwartest du z.B. von einem Brief?
10 Wenn du genaue Informationen in einem Text finden willst, kannst du ihn gezielt nach und nach durchgehen. Diese Fragen können dir helfen: Wo? / **Where?** Wann? / **When?** Was? / **What?** Wie? / **How?** Wer / **Who?**

A field trip

8a

Look at the text. What sort of text is it?
Circle the following information in the text:
· the writer of the text · the writer's address · who the text is written to

8b

Now read the text. Underline the following information about the field trip in the same colour: Where are the students going? When is the trip? When does it start and when do they plan to come back? Who cannot go on the trip? What must the students wear? What must they bring?

Holland Park School
Airlie Gardens, Campden Hill Rd
London W8 7AF

To: Year 8 parents
Dear parents,

I'm writing to inform you about our field trip to the British Wildlife Centre on 25th March.

The trip costs £15 for each student.

We are leaving by bus from the school's car park at 8am and are coming back at 6pm.

Please make sure that your child is wearing appropriate clothes (no school uniform, warm jacket, good shoes for walking). All students must bring a packed lunch and something to drink (no glass bottles, please). Please return the permission slip and pay the £15 by 15th March. We cannot take any students without payment and written permission! I am looking forward to an interesting and educational trip!

Yours sincerely,

R. Patel

PRACTISE READING

Haben **Tipps 4 und 10** dir geholfen, den Text zu verstehen? ○ ja ○ teilweise ○ nein

What, when, why?

9 CHOOSE YOUR LEVEL grammar: simple present questions TB p. 179

I Unscramble the questions.

1 the children · Where · are ______

2 is · What · job · Katy's ______

3 they · with the bees · starting · Are ______

II Unscramble the questions.

4 help · How · you · can · the hedgehogs ______

5 the centre · the bees · help · Does ______

6 hedgehogs · Where · sleep in the winter · do ______

III Unscramble the questions.

7 do you · what · a hammer · for · need ______

8 is it · the long grass · why · important · to check ______

9 at home · can · help · you · the bees ______

Challenge: Answer questions 3 to 9 in your exercise book.

Squirrels in the city

10 skill: mediation TB p. 155

Anna from Germany and her British friend Bella are looking at the squirrels in St James's Park. Read the dialogue. Then answer Bella's questions in English. Make notes first. Record yourself.

Anna: There are so many squirrels here in St James's Park! Are they all grey?
Bella: Yes, there are lots of squirrels in London, mostly grey ones. St James's Park is probably the best place for a *#squirrelselfie*, because there are so many tame ones[1]. You can feed them unsalted peanuts[2]. Have you got grey squirrels in Germany?
Anna: No. I don't think so. But my friend Lia has some squirrels in her garden. Look what she writes about them in her blog.

Bella's questions:

1 Are there any grey squirrels in her garden?
2 Are the squirrels as tame as here in St James's Park?
3 Oh, sweet – what does it do? Does it sit on her lap[3]?
4 Does Lia feed the squirrel? What does it eat?
5 OK, and what's its favourite food?
6 What else does she say about the squirrel?

In unserem Garten hinter dem Haus leben einige rote Eichhörnchen. Schwarze oder graue habe ich hier noch nie gesehen. Eins ist besonders zahm und kommt seit letztem Sommer jeden Tag zu mir. Wenn ich draußen sitze, frisst es mir nicht nur aus der Hand, sondern klettert auch an meinem Bein hoch und auf meinen Schoß. Es sitzt dort oft lange und frisst die Nüsse, die ich ihm gebe.
Ich liebe es, das Eichhörnchen zu füttern und ich habe ihm auch einen Namen gegeben. Es heißt Skippy. Ich finde, Eichhörnchen sind sehr süße, interessante und faszinierende Tiere. Sie dürfen nicht alles fressen, aber Nüsse sind okay. Skippy mag ungesalzene Erdnüsse besonders gern.

1 tame ones – zahme (Eichhörnchen), **2 unsalted peanuts** - ungesalzene Erdnüsse, **3 lap** – Schoß

An animal fact file

11 CHOOSE YOUR LEVEL

I Read about hedgehogs in TB7b again. Complete the fact file. II Read about bees in TB7b again. Complete the fact file. III Read Land & Leute 5 (TB p.72) again. Complete the fact file with five facts.

hedgehogs	bees	sea animals
a problem for hedgehogs:	what bees need to live:	sea animals that live in Britain:
what is difficult for them:	where bees live at the Centre:	where you can see dolphins:
what they need in winter:	how many species produce honey:	
what you can do to help them:	where bees live in nature:	
what you can feed them:	what you can do to help them:	

The children's project

12a audio 2/11

Listen to TB11b again. Read the sentences. Tick true or false.

		true	false
1	The reporter is in Hendon.	☐	☐
2	Lily and Tarek are planting flowers.	☐	☐
3	The children are helping the hedgehogs.	☐	☐
4	They had to ask before they started planting.	☐	☐
5	Everybody could plant flowers in London.	☐	☐
6	The reporter thinks that it's a good idea.	☐	☐

Challenge: Correct the false sentences in your exercise book.

12b media worksheet 5

Listen to TB11b again and look at the picture. Take notes.
Talk about the children's project and record yourself. Edit your recording.

You can say:

I can see …
The children are …
The reporter is …
Lily tells him …
Tarek talks about …

The children explain that …
On the Internet you can …
The reporter thinks that …
In the end he says that …

More about the garden arts and crafts

13 CHOOSE YOUR LEVEL skill: reading TB p. 154

I Read the sentences you wrote for TB12 again. Answer the questions.

1 What can you do with the wood, hammer and nails?

______________________________.

2 Where should you put the house?

______________________________.

3 What do you have to do to finish it?

______________________________.

II Read the sentences you wrote for TB12 again. Answer the questions.

1 What can you build with the wood, hammer and nails?

______________________________.

2 Where should you hang it?

______________________________.

3 What do you have to do last?

______________________________.

III Read the sentences you wrote for TB12. Answer the questions.

1 What do you need plates, water, dry leaves and dry flowers for?

______________________________.

2 Where should you put the plate overnight?

______________________________.

3 What can you do with the product in the end?

______________________________.

Sound check

14 audio 2/13

Learn to say the letters 'ou'. Listen to the words and repeat them. How many different pronunciations can you hear?

round · countryside · could · out · tour · dangerous · you · grounds · trouble · shout

Our environment brochure TARGET TASK SUPPORT

15 wordbank: wildlife TB p. 166, skill: writing TB p. 153

1 Collect ideas for a mini project that helps the environment.

2 Decide on one of the ideas.

3 Now collect information on your project. Write it down in keywords or sentences.

Why my project is good for the environment

What I need

Where I can do it

4 Create your page. Use your texts, add pictures and photos.

Tipp: Draft – edit – publish

Draft: Mache zunächst einen Entwurf *(draft)* für deine Seite. Skizziere hierfür den Aufbau der Seite auf einem separaten Blatt. Du kannst auch die einzelnen Elemente ausschneiden und hin- und herschieben.

Beachte dabei Folgendes:

Thema	Das Thema schreibst du in größerer, gut lesbarer Schrift oben auf dein Blatt.
Überschriften	Schreibe Überschriften über die einzelnen Texte oder Anleitungen auf deiner Seite.
Bilder	Achte bei der Auswahl der Bilder darauf, dass die Qualität gut ist.
Bildunterschriften	Schreibe Bildunterschriften unter deine Abbildungen.
Übersichtlichkeit	Deine Seite soll möglichst übersichtlich sein.

Edit: Überprüfe dann deinen Entwurf und verändere ihn, wenn nötig. Du kannst dies mit einem Partner/einer Partnerin besprechen.

Publish: Erst nach der Überarbeitung ist deine Seite fertig und kann veröffentlicht werden.

Die Check out-Seiten helfen dir einzuschätzen, was du schon gut kannst und was du noch üben solltest. Löse die Aufgaben auf dieser Doppelseite und male die Kreise wie auf Seite 20 rot, gelb oder grün aus.

1 Kannst du Schulregeln verstehen?
2 Kannst du deine Meinung zu Regeln formulieren?
3 Kannst du die Beschriftung eines deutschen Schildes auf Englisch wiedergeben?
4 Kannst du Flyer zu Ausflugszielen verstehen?
5 Kannst du einem Brief wichtige Informationen entnehmen?
6 Kannst du ein gehörtes Interview zusammenfassen?

1

Some of these rules are school rules and some aren't. Tick ✓ the school rules.

- ☐ Students must not be late.
- ☐ Eating snacks is allowed during lessons.
- ☐ Students must show respect to others.
- ☐ Students can't bring knives to school.
- ☐ On hot days, students can wear hats or caps.
- ☐ Students must hide their piercings.

Ich kann Schulregeln verstehen. ○

2

What do the children think about the rules? Complete their statements. Use the phrases in the box.

search the Internet · makes learning easier · important for our future job

Brendan: It's a good rule that we must be on time because that's also ____________.

Mia: I think we should be allowed to use mobile phones because then we could ____________

Eli: In my opinion we should be allowed to drink water during lessons because it ____________

Ich kann meine Meinung zu Regeln formulieren. ○

3

Tell an English family what the sign says.

Regeln auf dem Spielplatz Sonnenweide

- Der Spielplatz darf von Kindern unter 12 Jahren benutzt werden.
- Kinder unter drei Jahren dürfen den Spielplatz nicht allein betreten. Sie dürfen ihn nur in Begleitung von Erwachsenen oder Kindern älter als acht Jahre benutzen.
- Picknicks und Grillen sind nicht erlaubt.

Ich kann die Beschriftung eines deutschen Schildes auf Englisch wiedergeben. ○

4

Read the flyer and tick ✓ the correct statements.

Denham Country Park

Our large park is home to wildlife like water birds and insects and it offers fun activities for the whole family all year round. The playground is a great place for kids 12 years of age and younger. Walk or cycle along the rivers Colne and Misbourne, see the Grand Union Canal or visit beautiful Denham Village.

1 You can see wildlife like foxes and deer in the park.

2 You can only visit the park from spring to autumn.

3 Colne and Misbourne are villages.

4 The playground is not for kids over 12.

5 You can cycle in the park.

Ich kann Flyer zu Ausflugszielen verstehen.

5

Read the letter and tick ✓ true or false.

Dear parents,
We would like to invite you to our Year 8 Parents' Evening on Tuesday 15th April, from 5:30pm to 7:30pm. On this evening, you can talk to your child's subject teachers and also find out about some new projects at your school. Please use the Parent Mail System to let us know if you want to take part or call Ms Kelly at the school office.
Yours sincerely,
M. Watson

	true	false
1 The letter is an invitation.		
2 The Parents' Evening lasts three hours.		
3 The parents can talk to the headteacher.		
4 They can send an email to the school or call the school office to tell them if they are coming.		

Ich kann einem Brief wichtige Informationen entnehmen.

6 audio 2/14

Listen to an interview about a Wildlife Watch group and complete the sentences.

1 The children are ______ to ______ years old. 2 They do ______ activities together. 3 They learn about the ______. 4 They find out about ______ and ______ in the forest. 5 They make things from ______ like ______ feeders or insect ______. 6 They meet on the first ______ of each month.

Ich kann ein gehörtes Interview zusammenfassen.

Wenn du noch mehr üben möchtest, gehe zu Practise more – Unit 3. DIGITAL+

Practise reading

Tipps 1, 6 und 7

1 Bevor du einen Text liest, sieh dir die Überschrift an und überlege, worum es gehen könnte.
6 Versuche, die Wörter, die du nicht gleich verstehst, aus dem Textzusammenhang oder aus der Situation zu schließen. Nutze dabei nicht nur dein Allgemeinwissen, sondern auch deine sprachlichen Vorkenntnisse.
7 Es gibt viele Wörter, die im Englischen und im Deutschen ähnlich oder sogar gleich sind. Es kann dir helfen, nach solchen Wörtern zu suchen, wenn du einen Text liest.

A time capsule project

1a

What is a time capsule? Tick your answer.

☐ a special kind of clock ☐ a message in a bottle ☐ a container that you fill with objects of this time

1b

Read the flyer. What do you think these words mean? Check your answers in a dictionary.

take part
- ☐ einen Teil nehmen
- ☐ teilnehmen
- ☐ etwas abgeben

hand in
- ☐ die Hand geben
- ☐ einreichen
- ☐ mit den Händen in etwas hineinfassen

a public opening
- ☐ eine Öffnung vor Publikum
- ☐ ein offenes Loch
- ☐ eine große Öffnung

What will the future bring?
What are your dreams?

TAKE PART IN OUR SCIENCE MUSEUM TIME CAPSULE PROJECT!

What do you think:
what will life be like in 20 years' time?
What will the world look like?
What are your dreams for the future?

The Science Museum is inviting children between 6 and 14 to take part in our project.

Write about, draw, paint, film, ... your ideas about the future. How will we live, work, eat, learn, travel, ...?

We will show your works at the museum until 10 December. Then we will choose 15 of them that will stay at the museum after the exhibition.

We will then put these 15 works in a time capsule and there will be a public opening of the capsule in 20 years.

Please hand in your work by 26 May either online or at the museum!

1c

Which words are similar or even the same in English and in German? Write them in the lists.

English	German	English	German
bring			

PRACTISE READING

Haben **Tipps 1, 6 und 7** dir geholfen, den Text zu verstehen? ◯ ja ◯ teilweise ◯ nein

The children's future

2a CHOOSE YOUR LEVEL

I Read TB2b. Match ⁄ the questions and answers and write them in your exercise book.

1 What is Lily working on? — Ava.
2 What will happen with the capsule? — In a fancy flat in New York.
3 Who will be an engineer? — A collage for her project.
4 Where will Lily live in the future? — There will be a public opening in 20 years.

II Read TB2b. Answer the questions in your exercise book.

1 What can you hand in for the project?
2 How many works will they keep in the capsule?
3 Where will the capsule be for 20 years?
4 How can the museum contact the children?

III Read TB2b. Write the questions for these answers.

1 ______________________ It's about children's ideas about life in the future.
2 ______________________ She thinks they should not just write about jobs.
3 ______________________ His plan is to have his own restaurant.
4 ______________________ His hungry band mates.

2b

Read TB2b again. Complete the sentences.

1 For Lily's project you can hand in a ____________, a ____________, a ____________ or a story, whatever you like. 2 In 20 years the ____________ will be opened in a public ____________. 3 Tarek will be a famous ____________ in 20 years with his own ____________. 4 Harry will bring his ____________ mates after the concerts in ____________. 5 Lily asks the others to take part in the ____________, too. 6 Ava's idea is to also write about ____________, ____________ and ____________. 7 Tarek wants to ____________ food from the ____________. 8 Harry wants to ____________ a song with his ____________. 9 ____________ will to do something about technology in the future.

Sound check

3 audio 2/16

Practise some difficult words. Listen to the words and repeat.

time capsule · future · science museum · exhibition · mechanic · drawing · public opening · collage · fashion designer · engineer · technology · chef · restaurant

The future for Erin, Mike and Lou

4 grammar: will-future TB p. 186

Look at the pictures and talk about the children's ideas for the future. Take notes. Record yourself and edit the recording.

You can say: *Maybe Erin will be … She won't … I think Mike … Perhaps Lou …*

A good job

5a CHOOSE YOUR LEVEL grammar: comparison of adjectives TB p.177, wordbank: jobs TB p.167

Collect all the words for jobs you can find in your exercise book. Write about them. Use these adjectives.

bad · boring · clean · dangerous · difficult · dirty · fun · good · hard · helpful · important · interesting · useful · responsible[1] · simple[2] · well-paid[3]

1 **responsible** – verantwortungsvoll, 2 **simple** – einfach, 3 **well-payed** – gut bezahlt

I **Write more sentences like this.** *Being a hairdresser is hard. Being a vet is harder.*

II **Write more sentences like this.** *Being a football player is hard. Being a hairdresser is harder than being a football player. Being a vet is the hardest job.*

III **Write more sentences like this.** *Being a vet is more useful than being a mechanic. Being a doctor is the most useful job because …*

5b

Look at your collection of jobs. Answer the questions.

1 For which of the jobs do you need a uniform?

2 For which of the jobs do you have to study?

3 Which of the jobs do you do outside?

4 Which of the jobs do you do inside?

5 In which of the jobs can you be your own boss?

6 In which of the jobs can you be creative?

Challenge: **Think of three more questions for a partner.**

Four jobs

6a audio 2/18

Listen to the four people and number the pictures in the correct order.

6b

Write the words for the people's jobs under the pictures.

Perhaps you will be ...

7a grammar: will-future TB p. 186

Read the sentences. Write down what the person will be. Use 'I think', 'perhaps' or 'maybe'.

1 I like going to the drama club. *I think you will be an actor.*

2 I love animals. *Perhaps you*

3 I want to take care of ill people.

4 I want to help people in trouble.

5 I really like to bake bread.

6 I just love music.

7b

What do you like doing? What do you think you will be? Write sentences like those in 7a.

Challenge: **Write about two people you know. What do they like doing? What do you think they will be?**

Lots of jobs

8 CHOOSE YOUR TASK

A Find the job words in the snake. Write them in your exercise book.

B Work with a partner or in a group. One of you acts out a job and the other(s) guess(es) what it is.
C Write predictions[1] for a friend.
You can write: *I think that you'll be … I'm sure that you'll … Perhaps you won't … You will become …*

1 prediction – Vorhersage

A job in Germany

9 CHOOSE YOUR LEVEL skill: mediation TB p.155

Don, der Vater deines englischen Freundes, sucht Arbeit. Er würde dafür auch nach Deutschland umziehen. Du hast diese Anzeige in einer Zeitung gefunden und erzählst Don am Telefon davon. Beantworte I zwei oder mehr Fragen II drei oder mehr Fragen III die Fragen. Mache eine Aufnahme.

1 **Don:** Tell me about the job for an engineer.
2 **Don:** What kind of person are they looking for?
3 **Don:** What will my tasks be?
4 **Don:** But I don't live in Germany. Is that a problem?
5 **Don:** Where do I have to send my documents and what is the deadline?

Gesucht: Ingenieur (m/w/d)
Wir suchen für unseren Betrieb SolarTech in Köln zum nächstmöglichen Termin einen Ingenieur zur Unterstützung unseres Teams. Ihre Aufgaben sind das Installieren von Solarzellen auf Gebäuden aller Art.
Wir erwarten freundliche Mitarbeiter, die sich mit neuen Technologien auseinandersetzen möchten und keine Scheu vor Kundenkontakt haben.
Gute englische Sprachkenntnisse sind von Vorteil im Umgang mit unseren Kunden im europäischen Ausland.
Bei Bewerbungen aus dem Ausland stellen wir bei Bedarf eine Wohnung zur Verfügung. Wir bieten auch Bewerbungsgespräche per Webkonferenz an.
Wir freuen uns auf Ihre Bewerbung, die Sie bitte bis zum 1.5. an diese Zeitung senden. *Chiffre: HPD7765*

Long and short

10

Match the long and short forms. Write down the pairs. Check with your grammar pages.

~~it is~~ · you'll be · she is · they have not · he will not · I am · they don't · he'll · she has got · ~~it's~~ · they haven't · they are · she's got · they're · you will be · he will · he won't · she does not · they do not · she's · she doesn't · I'm

it is - it's

LANGUAGE HELP Das Futur mit will: Fragen TB. S. 187

In Entscheidungsfragen stellt du *will* an den Satzanfang. Beispiel: *Will you live in London?*
Die Kurzantworten lauten: *Yes, I will.* oder *No, I won't.*

Bei Fragen mit Fragewort steht das *will* nach dem Fragewort. Beispiel: *What will you be in the future?*
Bei verneinten Fragen ist es ebenso. Beispiel: *Won't you live in London? What won't you be in the future?*

Future questions

11 CHOOSE YOUR LEVEL

audio 2/20, grammar: will-future questions TB p.187

I Listen to TB11a again. Complete the questions and answer them.

1 Will Ava ______ in London? *Yes, she* ______

2 Will Ava ______ a pilot? ______

3 Will Ava ______ her skateboard? ______

4 Will Joshua ______ an engineer? ______

5 Will Joshua ______ a good vet? ______

II Listen to TB11a again. Complete the questions and answer them.

1 Will Ava ______ engineer? ______

2 Who will ______ Ava to the USA or Germany? ______

3 Will ______ a clown? ______

4 Who will ______ of ill animals? ______

5 Will ______ loads of pets? ______

III Listen to TB11a again. Unscramble the questions and answer them.

1 invent · will · things · Ava
2 Ava · to work · go · by car · will
3 what · to work · will · need to go · Ava
4 have · who · definitely · will · children
5 vet · Joshua · a good · will · be
6 won't · any · pets · why · Ava · have

My future

12

audio 2/21

Listen to the girl and answer the questions.

1 What will she be able to do when she is 18? *She will be able to* ______ .

2 How will she earn some money? *She will* ______ .

3 How will she travel? ______ .

4 What will she do when she comes back? ______ .

A class survey

13a CHOOSE YOUR LEVEL grammar: will-future questions TB p.187

Make a class survey about what you want to be in the future. First collect questions.

I Complete the questions with words from the box.

design · play · work · nurse · do · wear · live · designer · cut · firefighter · be · ...

1 Where will you ______ ?

2 Will you be a ______ ?

3 What will you ______ ?

4 Will you ______ cool clothes?

5 Will you ______ in a team?

II Complete the questions.

1 Where will you ...? 2 What will you ...? 3 What won't you ...? 4 Will you ...? 5 When will you ...?

III Write questions. Use the words in the box.

special clothes · team · earn · work with · be · firefighter · big company

13b wordbank: talking about the future TB p. 167

Now do the survey. Choose the best questions. Then ask your classmates. Take notes and tell the class about the answers.

You can say: *Roman thinks he will work in a big company. Tina says she will be an astronaut. Yussef thinks he won't be a nurse.*

Life in the future

14a

Sort the words from the box into the categories.

no cars · no exercise books · smart home · solar-powered helicopters · tablets · VR glasses · bikes · bigger TVs

travel	learning	houses
no cars	*no books*	

14b

Find more words for each category.

In the future, there will be – a new verse

15 audio 2/22-23

What do you want to have in the future? Write your own verses for the song. Record your version.

In the future, there will be a lot of ______ ,
lot of ______ , lot of ______ ,
in the future, there will be a lot of ______ .
Oh, the future will be wonderful.

In the future, there won't be a lot of ______ ,
lot of ______ , lot of ______ ,
in the future, there won't be a lot of ______ .
Oh, the future will be wonderful.

My ideas about the future TARGET TASK SUPPORT

16 wordbank: talking about the future TB p.167

1 Collect your ideas in a word web.

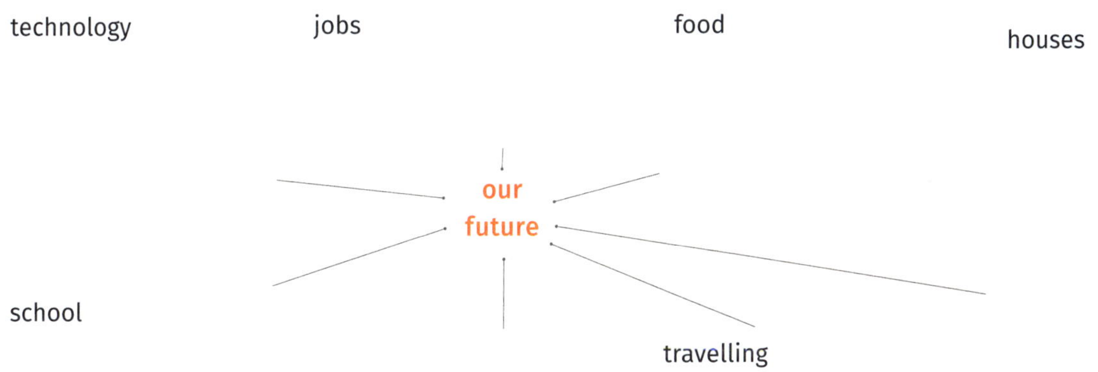

2 Complete the sentences. Choose the sentences you want to use in your presentation.

In the future, there will be ……

I think there won't be ……

I believe we will have ……

I hope we ……

My future ……

Everybody will ……

People ……

There won't be any ……

Most people won't have ……

My family ……

3 Use the space for a drawing or a first draft of your idea.

Tipp: Eine Zeitkapsel herstellen

Wenn deine Klasse sich entschließt, eine Zeitkapsel herzustellen, werden alle Ausstellungsstücke nach dem *gallery walk* in einen Behälter getan. Legt fest, wann der Behälter wieder geöffnet werden und wie die Öffnung geschehen soll. Welche Art von Behälter möchtet ihr verwenden? Wo soll er aufbewahrt werden? Eine Möglichkeit ist, ihn zu vergraben, eine andere, ihn so im Klassenraum aufzubewahren, dass die Klasse ihn nicht ständig sehen kann.

Um zu sehen, ob eure Ideen wahr geworden sind, müsstet ihr einige Jahre mit dem Öffnen warten. Dann seid ihr vielleicht nicht mehr als Klasse zusammen. Ihr könnt den Behälter aber auch am Ende des Schuljahres öffnen und euch an euren Arbeiten erfreuen. Ihr könnt dann auch überlegen, ob sich eure Vorstellungen von der Zukunft geändert haben.

Übrigens: Der Zeitpunkt der geplanten Öffnung wird auf den Behälter geschrieben.

Who says it?

1

Read the sentences from TB1b. Who says it? Write K for Kate or J for Jonathan next to the sentences.

1 Kate? Where are you? J
2 It has a really bright torch.
3 Can't you walk faster?
4 Watch out!
5 It looks like a tunnel.
6 It can read my messages to me.
7 Let's explore the old cellar.
8 It can also wake me up in the morning and give me directions.
9 Does it glow in the dark?

How do they talk?

2a audio 2/25, grammar: adverbs of manner TB p. 188

Listen to the sentences. How do Kate and Jonathan say these sentences? Write down what you think.

1 **Kate:** It looks like a tunnel. ______
2 **Jonathan:** Watch out! ______
3 **Kate:** Can't you walk faster? ______
4 **Kate:** Yeah, yeah, I'm being careful. ______
5 **Jonathan:** Oh. Spider. ______
6 **Kate:** I really wonder what we'll find. ______
7 **Kate:** Let me just see if ... ______
8 **Jonathan:** Kate? Where are you? ______
9 **Jonathan:** Look! It gives you the time, date and year. ______
10 **Kate:** We could check out that dark corner at the back. ______

slowly · excitedly · worriedly · loudly · fast · happily · angrily · calmly · sadly · proudly · nervously

2b CHOOSE YOUR LEVEL grammar: adverbs of manner TB p. 188

I Write four sentences.
II Write six sentences.
III Write eight or more sentences.

In her room In Kate's room In the cellar	Kate Jonathan	speaks shouts talks whispers asks ...	angrily. slowly. worriedly. proudly loudly. excitedly. fast. ...

2c grammar: adverbs of manner TB p. 188

Write down sentences. What can you say loudly, sadly, nervously, ...?

1 loudly: *I'm over here!*

2

3 sadly:

4

5 nervously:

6

7 :

8

How can you talk?

3a

Say each sentence in as many different ways as you can think of. Make a recording.

1 Great! Does it glow in the dark?
2 Let's explore the old cellar.
3 I really wonder what we'll find.
4 Oh. Spider.

3b

Get together in groups of three. Practise reading the story. You need a narrator, Kate and Jonathan. How does your character feel? Does he or she feel bored, angry, excited, happy, scared, ...?

What's the story like?

4

What do you think about part one of the story?

Make notes on the following questions:

1 Do you think the story is exciting?

2 Which scene is more exciting, in Kate's room or in the cellar?

3 What makes that scene more exciting?

4 Who is more scared, Jonathan or Kate?

5 How can you tell that Jonathan is a bit scared?

Adverb wordsnake

5 grammar: adverbs of manner TB p.188

Find the adverbs in the word snake.

The adventure – part two

6a

Look at the first part of the story in TB1b again. What do you think will happen next? Write sentences.

I think ______________________________

____

6b CHOOSE YOUR LEVEL audio 2/26

Listen to the story in TB4a again.

I Look at the pictures. Which of the things do you hear about in the story? Tick ✓.

1 
a spacecraft[1] ☐

2 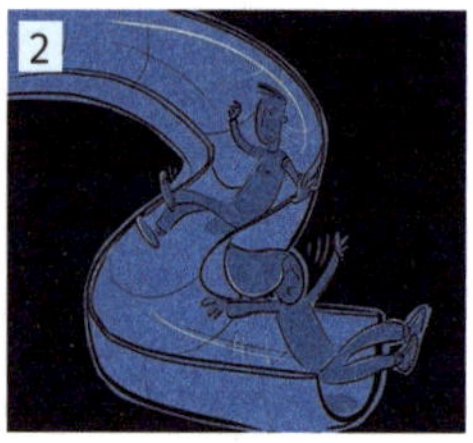
a slide ☐

3 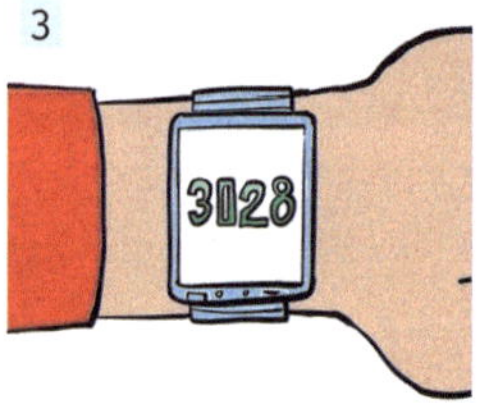

the year 3028 ☐

4 
a tunnel ☐

5 
an alien ☐

1 **spacecraft** – Raumfahrzeug

II Who does what? Complete the sentences with Jonathan, Kate, or Jonathan and Kate.

1 ______________ go down a huge slide.

2 ______________ is afraid.

3 ______________ wants to do it again.

4 ______________ looks at WatchIt 3000.

5 ______________ shuts up and finds out about the year.

III Correct the statements.

1 Jonathan looks for Kate in her house.

2 In the beginning, Jonathan thinks it's exciting.

3 Kate wants to go back to the river.

4 Jonathan tells Kate to look at his mobile phone.

5 Jonathan finds out that they are in the year 2028.

6c

Look at your ideas in 6a again. Were you right? Tick ✓.

☐ Yes, I was. ☐ No, I wasn't.

Practise reading

Tipps 3 und 8
3 Bei kurzen Texten unterstreiche alle Wörter, die du kennst. Bei längeren Texten unterstreiche nur die Wörter, die du nicht kennst. Manchmal erkennst du noch mehr Wörter, wenn du dir den Text anhörst. Unbekannte Wörter, die dir wichtig erscheinen, solltest du im Wörterbuch nachschlagen.
8 Es kann dir helfen, während des Lesens einen Text durch Unterstreichungen oder Markierungen zu strukturieren. Denke dabei daran, wer spricht oder denkt und achte auf Ortswechsel, Absätze und Sprechblasen.

Kate and Jonathan's adventure - part three

7a
audio 2/27

Underline all the words in the text you know. Use a pencil! Then listen to the audio. Do you understand more words now? Underline them, too. Look up the words you don't know.

7b

Underline in different colours: · the beginning of each new paragraph · what Jonathan says

☐ The children were quiet for a moment. Then they freaked out. When they were calm again, they sat down to think.

☐ Their first idea was to walk back into the tunnel and just go back in time. That did not work. There was something like a wall just inside the tunnel.

☐ Then they tried to change the year on Jonathan's watch but the watch simply changed it back to 2128. In the end they realized that they needed help. They walked towards Kate's house – or rather towards what used to be Kate's house.

☐ There it really became clear to them – in the place of her old red house stood something completely different. "Oh dear. We really ARE in the future." Jonathan said. They decided to hide in the bushes and find out who lived in the house now.

7c

Match the headings and the paragraphs. Write the numbers next to the paragraphs.

1 Kate and Jonathan's second idea
2 Kate and Jonathan realize where they are
3 Kate and Jonathan's first reaction
4 Kate and Jonathan's first idea

PRACTISE READING

Haben **Tipps 3 und 8** dir geholfen, den Text zu verstehen? ◯ ja ◯ teilweise ◯ nein

Five questions

8 CHOOSE YOUR LEVEL

Read TB 5b again. I Answer questions 1 and 2. II Answer questions 1, 2 and 3. III Answer the questions.

First paragraph
1 What do Kate and Jonathan try to get back home?
Second paragraph
2 How does Georgia know who Kate is?
Third paragraph
3 How do you know that Jonathan can go back in time with Kate?
Fourth paragraph
4 The children tell each other about their lives. What are the differences?
Fifth paragraph
5 What do Kate and Jonathan have to do now? Why?

Practise your style

9

grammar: adverbs of manner TB p. 188, linking words TB p. 189

1 **Complete the text with the correct numbers.**

1 slowly · 2 dark · 3 clearly · 4 single · 5 carefully · 6 big · 7 good · 8 old · 9 instantly

They knew every _4_ bit of the ___ cellar from their trips down there. Except this one ___ corner. The children walked down the stairs ___ . It was difficult to see ___ in the cellar. But when Jonathan switched on the torch, the cellar lit up ___ . There was a ___ hole in the corner. They went nearer to have a ___ look. Kate ___ put a foot in the tunnel.

2 **Complete the text with the correct numbers.**

1 so that · 2 or · 3 while · 4 and · 5 when

_5_ it began to get dark, Kate and Jonathan said that they should go back. They could go back through the tunnel without any problems ___ they were holding the compass. "Now we have to write that letter to Georgia ___ hide it together with the compass in the cellar, ___ Georgia can find it in the future." "Obviously it worked ___ we wouldn't be here."

Double consonants

10

Fill in the double consonants.

ss (2x) · ll (5x) · ff · nn · pp · rr (2x)

carefu ___ y	ce ___ ar	wo ___ ied	te ___ ibly
disa ___ ear	hi ___	bri ___ iant	di ___ icult
tu ___ el	compa ___	me ___ age	rea ___ y

Imagine you had a time machine

11 CHOOSE YOUR LEVEL video 11, skill: watching a video clip TB p. 156

Watch the video clip in TB10a. Take notes for I two of the children. II three of the children. III the children.

Name:	Time they want to travel to	Place they want to travel to	Why?	Other information
Ella	*the future in 300 years*	--	*she is curious, what will people invent?*	*bring some cool ideas back to the present*
Archie				
Emily				
Ben				
Casey				

A report on science fiction

12 audio 2/30, skill: mediation TB p.155

Listen to the radio report on science fiction. Your friend likes science fiction but doesn't understand everything. Help him or her to understand the report. Record your answers in German.

1 Was hat er über Fans von Science Fiction gesagt?
2 Wo wurden die Papiere gefunden?
3 Was denken sie, wer die Geschichten geschrieben hat?
4 Was wird bald passieren?

Sound check

13a audio 2/31

Listen to the words and repeat them.

~~rather~~ · ~~thank~~ · ~~next~~ · calm · technology · dark · transport · paragraph · ending · camera · present

13b

Listen again and fill in the lists.

/ɑː/	/æ/	/e/
rather	*thank*	*next*

13c audio 2/32

Listen again and check your lists.

More on science fiction

14 CHOOSE YOUR TASK

A **What do you think we will eat in the future? Make a drawing or a collage and label it.**
B **What do you think Kate and Jonathan will do when they visit Georgia? Write about it.**
C **Invent your own time machine. What does it look like? How do you travel with it? Make a drawing, label it or write about it.**

Visitors from space

15 CHOOSE YOUR LEVEL skill: writing TB p. 153

Answer the questions in your exercise book and you will get a story. You can look at the pictures for ideas or use your own ideas.

I

1 What day was it?
2 Where did the spacecraft[1] land?
3 What did the spacecraft look like?
4 Who was in the spacecraft?
5 What did the aliens[2] do?
6 Who did they meet?
7 What did the people do?
8 What did the aliens do next?
9 What happened in the end?

II

1 What day was it?
2 Where did the spacecraft[1] land?
3 What did the spacecraft look like?
4 Who was in the spacecraft? How many?
What did they look like?
5 What did the aliens[2] do first?
6 Who did they meet?
7 What did the people do?
What did they say?
8 What did the aliens do next?
9 What happened in the end?

III

1 What day was it?
2 Where did the spacecraft[1] land? What did it look like?
3 Who was in the spacecraft? How many?
What did they look like? How did they move?
4 What did the aliens[2] do first?
5 Who did they meet? What did the people do?
What did they say?
6 What did the aliens do next?
7 What did the people do then?
8 What did the aliens say to the people?
9 What did the people answer?
10 What happened in the end?

1 spacecraft – Raumschiff, **2 aliens** – Außerirdische

Challenge: **Read p. 153 in your textbook. Use the information to edit your text.**

My story TARGET TASK SUPPORT

16 wordbank: good style TB p. 169, skill: writing TB p. 153

1 What is your story about? Look at the pictures and notes for ideas. Tick ✓ the idea you like best.

☐ 

☐ 

☐
- a group of aliens
- land in German schoolyard
- 2035
- find new friends

☐
- me and my best friend
- travel to London
- 1523
- dirty and smelly

2 Plan your story. Organize your ideas.

Beginning: **Choose a first sentence. Complete it with your ideas and write it down.**

On a sunny day my friend Julian and I found a small metal box in our garden.

In the year 1983 / 2193 / ______

On a sunny / windy / cold / warm day ______

In our garden / At school ______

My friend Julian and I / An alien from space ______

Middle: **Structure[1] your ideas for the main part of the story. Add time words to your text.**

first, then, later, at ... o'clock, last weekend, in the morning, in the afternoon, after that

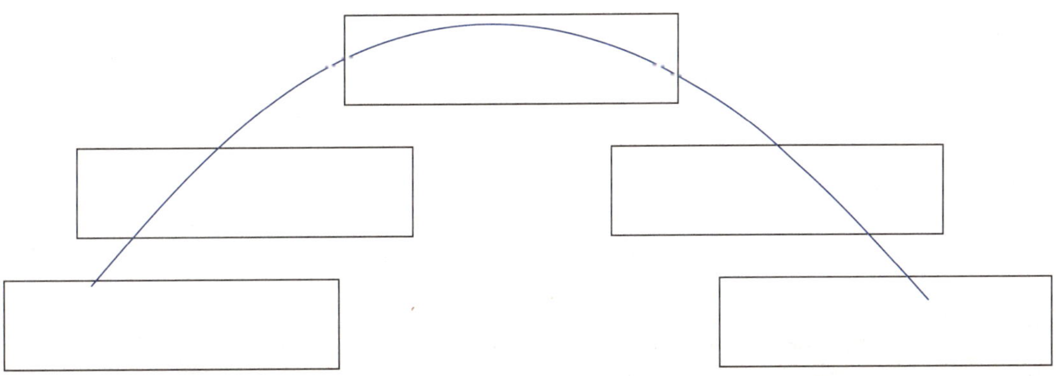

1 structure – strukturiere

Ending: **Write a good last sentence for your story.**

Finally / In the end / At last ______

Tipp: Eine Geschichte schreiben

1 Bevor du mit dem Schreiben der Geschichte beginnst, sammle deine Ideen immer schriftlich.
2 In die Einleitung gehören die Informationen zu *where, who, when*.
3 Der Verlauf einer Geschichte besteht aus Handlungsschritten. Achte darauf, dass diese logisch aufeinanderfolgen. Verknüpfe sie mit Zeit- und Verbindungswörtern.
4 Versuche deine Geschichte spannend zu gestalten, indem du sie auf einen Höhepunkt hin aufbaust.
5 Schreibe durchgehend in einer Zeitform (am besten im *simple past* oder *simple present*).
6 Runde deine Geschichte mit einem Schlusssatz ab.

Die Check out-Seiten helfen dir einzuschätzen, was du schon gut kannst und was du noch üben solltest. Löse die Aufgaben auf dieser Doppelseite und male die Kreise wie auf Seite 20 rot, gelb oder grün aus.

1 Kannst du einen Flyer über ein Projekt verstehen?
2 Kannst du darüber sprechen, wie sich Personen die Zukunft vorstellen?
3 Kannst du verstehen, was Leute über ihren Beruf sagen?
4 Kannst du darüber schreiben, wie jemand etwas tut?
5 Kannst du darüber schreiben, wie sich jemand fühlt?
6 Kennst du Möglichkeiten, eine Geschichte interessanter zu machen?

1

Read the flyer and tick ✓ the correct statements.

Kids' Project Week at the Willard Science Centre
Are you interested in how things work? Then join us for our science project week from August 12th to 16th. You will build simple machines, do amazing food science experiments, create new things from rubbish, learn about the stars and much more. There will be activities for different age groups (6–8 / 9–11 / 12–14).

1 The flyer is about a school project. ☐
2 It lasts five days. ☐
3 You can build things and do experiments. ☐
4 Children between 4 and 16 can take part. ☐

Ich kann einen Flyer über ein Projekt verstehen. ○

2 grammar: will-future statements TB p. 186

Write about the children's ideas for the future.

1 Bella: (+) be a zoologist in Africa, (–) come home very often

Bella thinks that she ____________________

2 Eddie: (–) stay in London, (+) move to Wales, have a farm

____

3 Lexi: (+) open her own baker's shop, (–) more than two children

____

Ich kann darüber sprechen, wie sich Personen die Zukunft vorstellen. ○

3 audio 2/33

Listen to four people talking about their jobs and complete the sentences.

1 Liz is a __________. She loves her job because she can __________
2 Ron is a __________. He loves his job because he can __________
3 Fatma is a __________. She loves her job because she can __________
4 Patrick is a __________. He loves his job because he can __________

Ich kann verstehen, was Leute über ihren Beruf sagen. ○

4

Complete the sentences with the words from the box.

angry · excited · surprised · terrible · worried

1 We're planning a birthday party for Albie at my place. He'll be so ______________!

2 Maisie feels ______________ because she has a conflict with her best friend.

3 At 9pm John still wasn't home yet and his mother felt really ______________.

4 When Harper broke her brother's new glasses, he was very ______________ with her.

5 The Millers want to change their house into a smart home and they feel really ______________ about it.

Ich kann darüber schreiben, wie jemand etwas tut.

5 grammar: adverbs of manner TB p. 188

Rewrite the sentences with the adverbs from the box.

carefully · easily · quickly · quietly · sadly

1 Logan ran to the bus stop. ______________

2 Elsie can repair things. ______________

3 The Blunts left their old home. ______________

4 The parents entered the baby's room. ______________

5 Please carry these new plates. ______________

Ich kann darüber schreiben, wie sich jemand fühlt.

6 grammar: adverbs of manner TB p. 188; linking words TB p. 189

Rewrite the sentences to make them more interesting. Use the words in brackets.

1 Rory woke up yesterday. He felt excited. It was his birthday. (when · very · because)

When Rory ______________

2 He got up. He went to the living room. No one was there. (quickly · and · but)

____

3 Rory got sad. The door opened. His family came in. (really · but · suddenly · and)

____

4 They gave him a baby dog for a present. He was happy for the rest of the day. (white · so · very)

____

Ich kenne Möglichkeiten, eine Geschichte interessanter zu machen.

Wenn du noch mehr üben möchtest, gehe zu Practise more – Unit 4. DIGITAL+

Interesting places you know

1

Talk to your partner about interesting places you know. Use your list from TB1.

You can say:

I know the … museum.
There you can see …
We sometimes go to …
I don't know much about …
I think … sounds really interesting.
At the … you can learn about …
I have been to …
I want to see the …

LANGUAGE HELP Große Zahlen auf Englisch schreiben

Im Englischen benutzt man gerne Kommas, um Zahlen mit vier oder mehr Stellen besser lesbar zu machen.
Beispiel: 50,000 statt 50000 Aber: Bei Angaben von Jahreszahlen wird kein Komma verwendet. Beispiele: 1957, 2017

Discover the information

2

What can you see at the museums in TB2a? Sort the words from the box into the lists.

modern trainers · mummy of a cat · Dr Watson · glasses · violin · Egyptian hieroglyphs · old Egyptian shoes · pipe collection · desk · theatre and musical costumes · hats · microscope

The British Museum	The Victoria and Albert Museum	The Sherlock Holmes Museum

Challenge: What do the numbers stand for?

2,000 · 4,000 · 19th · 3,000

2,000

Sherlock Holmes and Dr Watson

3a

Read about Sherlock Holmes and the museum in TB2a and 3a again. Take notes.

Challenge: What do you know about Dr Watson?

3b media worksheet 5

Now talk about your notes. Talk for 40 seconds or longer. Make a recording and edit it.

You can say: *At 221B there is … It is not a normal museum because … Holmes didn't really … The museum is about … At the museum you can see … … just a character from a book.*

What they have done

4 grammar: present perfect statements TB p.190

Read the sentences from TB3a. Cross out the green phrases and replace[1] them with phrases you like.

I've just looked at ~~my watch~~ *a picture* ______. I've found it ______. Haven't you been to enough museums ______? Have you ever seen a shoe that is 3,000 years old ______? I've never been there ______. I've found something else – the Sherlock Holmes Museum ______. ______. We've read a story about him ______.

1 **(to) replace** – ersetzen

Signal words

5 CHOOSE YOUR LEVEL grammar: present perfect statements TB p.190

I Read TB3a again. Match ⁄ the sentence parts.

1 Ava has never seen
2 Harry has already read
3 In the flyer they have put
4 Tarek has actually seen

together lots of interesting information.
a mummy before.
a story about Sherlock Holmes.
a collection of old shoes before.

II Complete the sentences. Use the words in brackets and put them into the present perfect.

1 The children *have* just *looked* (look) at the museum flyer.
2 Harry ______ (not see) the home of a detective yet.
3 Ava and Noah ______ (be) to five museums so far.
4 I ______ already ______ (check) my weather app twice today. I think it will rain.

III Write four sentences in your exercise book.

read one of Sir Arthur Conan Doyle's books.	play the violin.	4 Lily	find a flyer about museums.
yet.	never	not look through a microscope	2 Lily and Harry
just	1 Ava	3 Tarek	already

You can write: *Ava has never …*

Inside the museum

6 grammar: present perfect statements TB p.190

Read TB6a again. Write five sentences.

I've read	his violin next to his desk.
	wax models all over the house.
They've put	that funny hat on his head.
	a newspaper on his desk.
They've left	about that.

Let's go to the museum

7 CHOOSE YOUR LEVEL skill: mediation TB p.155

You are in London with a friend who does not speak English very well. He sees these museum flyers. Answer his questions in German in your exercise book.

The Horniman Museum

Are you interested in animals? Come to the Horniman Museum and see the big collection of stuffed animals. But there's more: you can learn a lot about natural history and enjoy the gallery of musical instruments, too.

- **Where?** Forest Hill
- **What?** Natural history, musical instruments and a large collection of stuffed animals
- **How much is it?** Free, except for special exhibitions and events

The Tate Modern

Are you an art lover? At the Tate Modern you can look at modern and present art works. It's one of the most visited museums in Britain. Come by and enjoy masterpieces by Andy Warhol or Picasso.

- **Where?** Bankside (with a lovely view of the Thames)
- **What?** Modern and present art from around the world
- **How much is it?** Free, except for special exhibitions and events

The Science Museum

Are you interested in exploring space, electricity, engines, or technology? Then you must visit the Science Museum. The best thing is that you can try some things yourself at the Wonder Lab.

- **Where?** Kensington and Chelsea
- **What?** Science, technology and industry
- **How much is it?** Free, except for special exhibitions and events

The London Transport Museum

Have you ever seen one of the famous red buses? Of course you have. But there is so much more to London Transport! At the museum you can learn all about the history of horse-drawn buses, trains, and the London Underground. There is also Harry Beck's original design from 1931 for his revolutionary system to draw the Underground map.

- **Where?** Covent Garden
- **What?** All about London's buses, trains and the Underground
- **How much is it?**
  Adults – £18.50
  Children and young people 17 and under – free

Answer four questions. Answer six questions. Answer the questions.

1 Welche der Museen kann man kostenlos besuchen?
2 Ich interessiere mich für ausgestopfte Tiere. Wo gehe ich am besten hin?
3 Ich möchte in ein Museum, das besonders berühmt ist und wo sehr viele Leute hingehen. Welches wäre das?
4 Ich würde mir auch gerne moderne Kunst anschauen. Wo kann ich hingehen?
5 Und wenn ich Kunst aus aller Welt sehen möchte? Wohin gehe ich dann?
6 Ich würde gerne etwas über Technologie lernen. Gibt es da auch etwas?
7 Mich interessieren auch alte Fahrzeuge von früher. Wo kann ich die sehen?
8 Es wäre auch toll, einen schönen Ausblick auf die Themse zu haben. Ist das irgendwo möglich?
9 Und wo kann man spezielle Ausstellungen ansehen?

Lots of museums

8 CHOOSE YOUR TASK

C: media worksheet 4

A **Look through the pages of TB Unit 1 and 5. Collect the names of all the museums you can find. What can you see or do there? Make notes.**

B **Would you go to a museum when you are on holiday in London? Why? Why not? Write about it.**
You can write: *There are so many very cool museums. I would like to go to … because …*

C **Find out more about the overstuffed walrus at the Horniman Museum. Make notes and tell your class about it.**

Sound check

9a

audio 3/3

Learn to say the letter 'v'.
Listen to the words and repeat them.

visit · Victoria · detective · violin · solve · overstuffed · vehicle · creativity · everyday

9b

Think of more words with the letter 'v'. Write them down in your exercise book and practise saying them.

A museum of everyday objects

10

audio 3/5

Listen to TB9a again and tick ✓ the correct answer.

1 What did Ava like best about the museum?
- [ ] She was allowed to touch everything.
- [ ] It wasn't so boring.
- [ ] She was allowed to sit on the chairs.

2 Tarek thinks it's a nice idea to
- [ ] take pictures at the museum.
- [ ] put normal things in a museum.
- [ ] put unusual things in a museum.

3 When Lily looks at her first lamp
- [ ] she thinks of designing a new lamp.
- [ ] she thinks of her time in Brighton.
- [ ] she wants to buy a new lamp in Brighton.

4 The children want to have an exhibition
- [ ] that looks like someone's home.
- [ ] for old things.
- [ ] for normal things that are special to them.

LANGUAGE HELP — Das Partizip Perfekt

Das Partizip Perfekt ist die dritte Form in der Verbtabelle. Bei regelmäßigen Verben bildest du es mit dem Infinitiv + *-ed*. Beispiel: Infinitiv: *clean* einfache Vergangenheit: *cleaned* Partizip Perfekt: *cleaned* Bei unregelmäßigen Verben musst du die Formen wie Vokabeln auswendig lernen. Beispiel: Infinitiv: *see* einfache Vergangenheit: *saw* Partizip Perfekt: *seen*

Lots of verbs

11 grammar: present perfect TB p.190

Are the verbs in the box regular or irregular verbs? Sort the verbs into the lists. Add the past participle.

~~use~~ · ~~do~~ · put · play · tell · smile · touch · walk · see · find · step · make · look · eat

regular verbs: infinitive	regular verbs: past participle	irregular verbs: infinitive	irregular verbs: past participle
use	*used*	*do*	*done*

LANGUAGE HELP — Das Perfekt: Fragen TB S. 191

Entscheidungsfragen im Perfekt bildest du, indem du *have* oder *has* an den Satzanfang stellst.
Beispiele: *Have you done your homework? Yes, I have. Has Jill done her homework? No, she hasn't.*
Bei Fragen mit Fragewort steht das Fragewort am Satzanfang. Beispiele: *What have you done? Why hasn't he gone home?*

What have you done?

12a grammar: present perfect TB p.190

Read the song in TB11a again. Which of the things haven't you done? Say why you would like to do them. Write five sentences or more in your exercise book.

You can write: *I have never been to Paris but I would like to go because* ______

______

12b CHOOSE YOUR LEVEL

Read the questions. Write short answers.

I Answer questions 1-3.
II Answer questions 2-5.
III Answer the questions.

1 Have you ever eaten snake?
2 Have you ever been at home for the holidays?
3 Have you ever had too much cake?
4 Have your friends ever done a marathon?
5 Has your teacher ever been to London?
6 Has your mum ever been to Rome?

1 *No, I* ______
2 ______
3 ______
4 ______
5 ______
6 ______

Practise reading

Tipps 2 und 9
2 Wenn es zu einem Text Bilder gibt, sieh sie dir an. Sie können dir Hinweise auf den Inhalt geben.
9 Überfliege den Text und suche gezielt nach Wörtern und Aussagen, die zu den Bildern passen. Du brauchst beim Überfliegen nicht jedes Wort zu lesen.

An exhibition of everyday things

13a

Look at the pictures. What do you think the texts are about?

A This beautiful vase is Grandma Edyta's masterpiece. You can see two painted roses – Edyta's favourite flowers – on the vase. She sculpted the vase in a workshop in 2022. It is 40cm high and weighs 2.3kg

B Lily designed this lamp when she still lived in Brighton. She used aluminium, plastic, and her creativity. The modern and functional design makes it special. It is 38cm tall and weighs 1.3kg

C These pink trainers with white stripes on their sides play an important role in Mrs Kogan's life. She wore these trainers when she ran her first marathon in 2013. Mrs Kogan is a great athlete now and has run many marathons since 2019. The trainers are size six and weigh 280g.

D This is Harry's first guitar. It is a wooden guitar for children. Harry played his first tunes on this instrument when he was five years old. Everybody could hear that there was a lot of musical talent in Harry. The guitar is green. It is 62cm long and weighs 510g.

13b

Now scan the texts. Which words fit the pictures? Underline the texts with two colours.
Colour 1: facts about the objects (weight / age / material / what it looks like)
Colour 2: background information (Who made it or used it? What makes it special?)

PRACTISE READING

Haben **Tipps 2 und 9** dir geholfen, den Text zu verstehen? ◯ ja ◯ teilweise ◯ nein

At an exhibition of everyday life

14a CHOOSE YOUR LEVEL

I Write down the correct words to describe the doll[1].

300 years old	brown eyes
long brown hair	pink lips
white shoes	40cm tall
blue dress	only one eye

1 **doll** – Puppe

II Look at the fact sheet for the skateboard.
Write a description in your exercise book.

two months old
red with yellow flames
four yellow wheels
very light[1]
great for practising tricks

1 **light** – leicht

III Look at the words in the box.
Which object can you describe with them?
Write a description in your exercise book.

ancient	souvenir from Spain
shiny	blue and silver[1]
beautiful	small and light[2]

1 **silver** – silbern; Silber, 2 **light** – leicht

14b audio 3/7

Listen to the guide at the exhibition of everyday life. Tick the object he is talking about.

☐ 

☐ 

☐ 

Sound check

15a audio 3/8

Learn to say the letter 'a'. Listen and repeat the words. How many different pronunciations[1] can you hear? ☐

had · mechanic · ancient · far · art · announcement · all · newspaper · call · take · market · that

15b

Listen again. Underline the words with the /eɪ/ sound as in 'make'.

1 **pronunciation** – Aussprache

15c audio 3/9

Listen and check your words.

Our exhibition of everyday objects TARGET TASK SUPPORT

16 skill: writing TB p. 153

1 Have you decided what sort of objects you want to show in class? Write down all the objects you think would be interesting to show. Then decide which one you want to describe.

objects that would be interesting to show	the object I want to describe

2 Complete the sentences. Then choose the sentences you want to use.

☐ This is my ______ ☐ It is ______ years old.

☐ It is ______ cm high and weighs ______ kg. ☐ It is made of[1] ______

☐ It is special to me because ______

☐ I use it to ______

☐ I made it at ______

☐ I made it when I was ______

☐ I got it for ______

☐ It is the ______ he wore when ______

☐ She bought it when ______

☐ It has been in the family for ______ years. ☐ Her ______ gave it to her.

☐ We used it for ______

☐ When you look at it closely, you'll see ______

1 **(to) be made of** – bestehen aus

Tipp: Informationstexte für eine Ausstellung schreiben

1 Wähle einen Gegenstand aus, der für dich besonders ist und über den du ein paar Dinge weißt.
2 Überlege: Welche Informationen findet man üblicherweise in einem Museum über die Ausstellungsstücke? Zum Beispiel: Von wem wurde es hergestellt? Wann und wo? Aus was ist es gemacht? Wie groß ist es?
3 Notiere diese Informationen über deinen Gegenstand in Stichpunkten.
4 Nimm ein schönes Blatt und schreibe deinen Informationstext in sauberer Handschrift darauf.

Holiday activities

1a

Look at the pictures of holiday activities. What do they make you think of? Make notes.

1

2

3

4

1b

Read the notes about the workshops in TB1. Match / the sentence parts.

1 The climbing workshop
2 I would choose the upcycling workshop
3 Two weeks of football
4 Writing a new version of a play
5 Climbing and action
6 I don't really like
7 I think I would go to the drama workshop
8 I would go to the football workshop

because I like ghost stories.
are not my thing.
because I like making things.
sounds really interesting.
because I want to get better at playing football.
sounds terrible to me.
creating things.
sounds a bit boring to me.

1c

Read the notes in TB1 again. What sounds interesting to you? What doesn't? Write about it.

What are they going to do?

2 CHOOSE YOUR LEVEL grammar: going to-future statements TB p. 192

Read TB2a. Write I four sentences II six sentences III nine sentences in your exercise book.

Ava
Tarek
Lily
Harry
Lily and Ava
At the drama workshop they
...

is going to
isn't going to
are going to

go to the hockey camp.
be on stage in a real theatre.
watch the performance.
act.
join the upcycling workshop.
go to Poland for two weeks.
do another cooking workshop.
create new things out of old stuff.
create a new version of the play.
...

LANGUAGE HELP — Das Futur mit going to: Fragen TB. S. 193

Bei Fragen mit Fragewort im going to-future steht das Fragewort an erster Stelle.
Beispiele: *What are you going to do in the holidays? When is the workshop going to start?*

What is going to happen?

3 grammar: going to-future questions TB p. 193

Read TB2a again. Complete the questions with the correct question words.

Where · What · Who · When · Why

1 ________ is Lily going to bring to the workshop?
2 ________ is Ava going to go on her holiday?
3 ________ is Ava going to go to Poland?
4 ________ isn't Tarek going to go to hockey camp?
5 ________ is not going to act?

Challenge: Write the answers in your exercise book.

Workshop words

4

Find the words in the word snake and write them down.

ACTION|RUBBISHCOURSEARTYOUTHACTIVITYDRAMAPROGRAMMECOACHPERFORM

Sound check

5a audio 3/11

Listen to the words in the lists and repeat them.

5b

Do you hear /tʃ/ or /dʒ/? Listen again and tick ✓ the correct sounds.

	/tʃ/	/dʒ/
adventure		
German		
lunchtime		
children		
enjoy		
choose		

	/tʃ/	/dʒ/
jump		
hedgehog		
China		
subject		
picture		
chain		

5c audio 3/12

Listen and check your lists.

A short version of the story

6 audio 3/13

Listen to TB7b again. Put the sentences of the short version of the ghost story in the correct order. Compare your version with a partner.

☐ The ghost wants them to move out again because it is his house.
☐ The ghost tries again and again and again and it's just not working.
☐ But the family is just not scared of ghosts.
☐ So he tries to scare them away but no one in the family is afraid of him.
☐ The Canterville ghost lives in a very old house in the country.
☐ One day, a family moves into the house: Mr and Mrs Otis and the twins, David and Jack.
☐ He gets really angry and frustrated and tries all sorts of scary things.

Something new for Harry

7 CHOOSE YOUR LEVEL audio 3/13

Listen to TB7b again.

I Are the sentences true or false? Tick ✓.

		true	false
1	Harry wants to act in the play.	☐	☐
2	Gus, the workshop leader, is an American guy.	☐	☐
3	There is no email address on the website.	☐	☐
4	Tarek and Harry don't know Gus.	☐	☐
5	The ghost story is very boring.	☐	☐

II Correct the false sentences.

1 The website says they need people for music and light. ______
2 Harry can sign up for the workshop online. ______
3 They can't find the email address. ______
4 Harry doesn't remember Gus. ______
5 At first, Harry thinks that the story sounds boring. ______

III Correct the false sentences.

1 Harry wants to be on stage with Tarek. ______
2 Everybody has to sign up by tomorrow. ______
3 Gus is an American guy they don't know. ______
4 There is no email address for Gus on the website. ______
5 Gus teaches a guitar masterclass. ______
6 Harry feels motivated[1] by the things Tarek says. ______

1 **feel motivated** – sich motiviert fühlen

The drama workshop

8 grammar: going to-future questions TB p. 193

Look at the pictures. What are the people going to do? What aren't they going to do? Write questions and short answers in your exercise book. You can write: *1 Is Harry going to act on stage? – No, he isn't.*

1 act on stage

2 do something with sound

3 look at the website

4 laugh about the story

5 do the guitar course

6 write an email to Gus

7 scare the Otis family

8 watch the performance

Gus' email to Harry

9

Read TB8 again. Help Gus to write his email to Harry. Underline the correct words. Then write the complete email in your exercise book.

1 Dear Harry, I remember you and your cousin / Tarek / your rabbit from the drama project / climbing worshop / football course at your school last year.

2 It was good of you to tell me about the deadline / take part in the workshop / write to me after the deadline.

3 There were no places left / many places left / a few places left until this morning, when one girl called me to say she couldn't come.

4 You can come to the course next summer / take her place now / write again tomorrow.

See you soon! Gus

At the start of the workshop

10 CHOOSE YOUR LEVEL audio 3/14

Listen to Gus and the children at the start of the workshop.

Read the sentences and tick ✓ true or false.

	true	false
1 Matt's teacher said that acting would be good for him.	☐	☐
2 Polly doesn't really like acting.	☐	☐
3 Tarek checked the information about the workshop on the website.	☐	☐
4 Tarek is doing the drama workshop because Harry told him about it.	☐	☐

II Complete the sentences.

1 Matt's teacher said that acting ______________ . 2 Polly read the play at school and would like ______________ . 3 Tarek took part in the drama project and ______________ .

4 Gus is not sure if they are going ______________ .

III Fill in the table with the names Harry, Polly, Matt and Tarek and the information from the dialogue.

Name:				
reason for joining the drama workshop		*is a bit shy[1], teacher said acting would be good*	*Tarek talked him into joining, he talked until Harry said yes*	

1 **shy** – schüchtern, scheu

Lots of ideas

11 media worksheet 5

Look at the picture. Where are Gus and the children? What are they talking about? What are they planning to do? Talk about the picture and record yourself. Edit your recording.

You can say:

Gus and the children are sitting on the stage.
There are ... children.
I think they are talking ...
They are planning ... They are discussing ...
They are going to need ... They will ...

At the theatre

12 CHOOSE YOUR TASK A, C: media worksheet 4

A **Which jobs are there at a theatre?** You can write: *An actor acts in a play. Then you need people for ...*
B **Would you like to act in a play? Why? Why not? Write about your ideas.**
C **Do you know any plays? Choose one. What is it about? Make notes.**

Practise reading

Tipps 4 und 8

4 Denk nach, bevor du liest. Oft ist es hilfreich zu überlegen, was du schon über ein Thema weißt, bevor du einen Text darüber liest. Überlege auch, was du über eine bestimmte Textsorte schon weißt – was erwartest du zum Besipiel von einer Gespenstergeschichte?
8 Es kann dir helfen, vor dem Lesen den Text durch Unterstreichen oder Markieren zu strukturieren. Denke dabei daran, wer spricht oder denkt und achte auf Ortswechsel, Absätze und Sprechblasen.

The Canterville Ghost

13a

Before you read the play, think about the story. What do you remember? Read the very short version of the story in WB6 again.

13b

Structure the text. Underline the following information with different colours:

- the different scenes
- where the scenes take place
- who is talking
- how the people are talking
- the sounds people and things make

SCENE 1: In front of the house

The Otis family arrives at Canterville House

Mrs Otis: This is our new home.

The twins: Ohhh! Is there a ghost here?

Mr Otis: No. There are no ghosts here! Ghosts don't exist.

Sir Simon: What? I don't exist? What rubbish! I'll show these people what a scary ghost I am.

SCENE 2: In the twins' bedroom

Sir Simon: *(rattles his chains)* Aahhh! I am the ghost of Sir Simon de Canterville. This is my house. Go away and never come back. Aaaah!

David: *(in a sleepy voice)* What's all this noise? We want to sleep!

Jack: *(bored)* Go away, Mr Ghost. We're tired.

Sir Simon: *(disappointed)* Right, I'll have to be even scarier tomorrow.

SCENE 3: In Mr and Mrs Otis' bedroom

(sound) CLANG, CLANG, CLANG

Sir Simon: *(nervous)* For 300 years I have lived in this house. Everyone was afraid of me. *(loud)* Wake up! I am the ghost of Canterville House!

Mrs Otis: Excuse me, Mr Ghost, please stop making all that noise.

Mr Otis: We can't sleep.

Sir Simon: *(angry, frustrated)* It's impossible to live in the same house as this family!

SCENE 4: On the stairs

(sound) CLONK, CLONK, CLONK

Sir Simon: I'm going to frighten everybody in this family. First the twins, then Mrs Otis. And of course Mr Otis ... I must practise my terrible laughter. Haaa. Haaaa. Haaa.

Mr Otis: What's all this about?

David: Go away!

Jack: And let us get back to sleep.

Sir Simon: Haaaa! My terrible laughter will frighten you away and ... *(stumbles)*

(sound) CRASH!

Otis family: Hahaha!

SCENE 5: Somewhere in the house

Sir Simon: These people are not afraid of me. I'm not a good ghost.

(Enter Mr and Mrs Otis)

Mrs Otis: Oh you poor thing. Why are you crying?

Sir Simon: I'm sad. I can't stay here if you're not afraid of me. The ghost inspector will find out and I will have to leave.

Mr Otis: Don't worry. We'll help you so that you can stay here. Where are the twins?

SCENE 6: Somewhere in the house

The ghost inspector has arrived

Sir Simon: *(rattles his chains)* BOO!

David and Jack: *(run away)* Aaaah!

Sir Simon: *(shows his terrible laughter)* Haaa. Haaaa. Haaa.

Mrs and Mrs Otis: Help!

Ghost inspector: Well done, Sir Simon. Very scary. You may stay at Canterville House. Goodbye.

David: Is he gone?

Sir Simon: Yes, I think he's gone.

The family and Sir Simon: Yipppeeeee!

PRACTISE READING

Haben **Tipps 4 und 8** dir geholfen, den Text zu verstehen? ◯ ja ◯ teilweise ◯ nein

How does the story end?

14 skill: writing TB p. 153

What do you think will happen after scene 6? Write an ending to the play. Choose some of the following ideas or think of your own. Then write scene 7 and read it to a partner. Get some feedback.

- [ ] Sir Simon is very tired now and needs some sleep.
- [ ] The family and Sir Simon are having a party.
- [ ] Other friendly ghosts come to live with the family.
- [ ] The twins want to celebrate that Sir Simon can stay.
- [ ] The house becomes a ghost museum.
- [ ] People come to the museum to see a real ghost.

After the performance

15 CHOOSE YOUR LEVEL skill: mediation TB p. 155

Am Tag nach der Aufführung erscheint diese Rezension in der Notting Hill Zeitung. Hilf einer deutschen Familie, die das Stück sehen möchte, zu verstehen, was in der Zeitung gesagt wird.

I Answer four questions.
II Answer six questions.
III Answer the questions.

1 Ist es die bekannte Version von Canterville Ghost?
2 Wie viele Schauspieler spielen mit?
3 Welche Rollen gibt es in dem Stück?
4 Ist das Stück sehr dramatisch oder traurig?
5 Gibt es besondere Klangeffekte?
6 Wie hat das Publikum reagiert?
7 Wird es eine weitere Vorstellung geben? Wo wird diese stattfinden?
8 Wie lange dauert die Vorstellung und was kostet der Eintritt?
9 Wer hat das Ganze geleitet?

A new version of an old play

Last night a group of very talented young people from Notting Hill performed a new version of *The Canterville Ghost* at the youth club. With the help of drama teacher Gus Graham they wrote their own very funny version. Tarek Adil and Matt Ross were very convincing as the twin brothers David and Jack. Marc King and Ella Sera were great parents. Helen Goodwin was the very strict ghost inspector. But the best actor that night was Polly Walsh. Her presentation of the ghost Sir Simon was so funny, the audience couldn't stop laughing. Especially important for the success of the play was the sound. It was lucky that Harry Norris was on the team. He did an excellent job. He made the ghost and his rattling chains sound very scary. There was a lot of applause. The audience was enthusiastic. They wouldn't stop cheering and clapping. Gus Graham promised that there is going to be another performance soon at the Rainbow Theatre.
Some important details for you: the performance lasts 1 hour 35 and tickets cost £5.

Silly tongue twisters

16a audio 3/16

Listen to the silly tongue twisters[1]. Practise saying them. Choose one and learn it by heart.

Seven sweet spiders sing some silly songs.

Fit black bats fly faster than fat black bats.

Ten tall tigers take twelve tomatoes to town.

16b

Write your own tongue twister. All words must start with the same letter or a combination of two letters. Consonants like b, g, l, s or t are a good idea.
Practise saying your tongue twister. Start slowly, then say it faster and faster. You can make a recording. Use the tongue twisters to warm up before acting.

1 **tongue twister** – Zungenbrecher

Our play TARGET TASK SUPPORT

17 skill: performing a scene TB p. 159

1 What is important for a play? Collect ideas.

props · costumes · music · sound · ...

2 What is the role of sound effects and music in a play? Tick ✓ your answers.

1 Sound effects and music add to the effect the play has on the audience. ☐

2 Sound effects must be scary for the audience. ☐

3 Music can can distract[1] from the action on stage. ☐

4 The actors can also make sounds and music. ☐

5 The music and sound should be louder than the actors. ☐

1 **(to) distract** – ablenken

A mini theatre dictionary

actor/actress - Schauspieler/in
audience - Publikum
drama - Schauspiel
effect - Effekt, Wirkung
(to) perform - aufführen
performance - Aufführung
play - Theaterstück
prompter - Souffleur/ Souffleusse
prop - Requisite
rehearsal - Probe
sound effects - Klangeffekte
stage - Bühne
voice - Stimme

3 Practise your stage voice.

- At home, practise speaking loudly and clearly.
- Pronounce all the consonants.
- Speak in front of a mirror.
- Record yourself.
- Stand in a corner of a room. Imagine you speak to someone standing in another corner.
- Say some tongue twisters.

Finally, get together with a partner and read scene 3 on page 120 of your textbook to each other. One of you reads the role of Sir Simon, the other one the roles of Mr and Mrs Otis. Speak slowly and clearly. Your partner has to understand everything you say.

4 After the rehearsal, give feedback to the other actors. You can use the phrases below.

- You played your role very well.
- Could you try to speak more slowly?
- You should come to the front of the stage.
- Speak up, please.
- You are good to understand.
- I can't see you, can you come to the front, please?

Tipp: Wie eine Aufführung gelingt

1 Überlegt euch, welches Stück ihr spielen möchtet (falls ihr euch nicht für *The Canterville Ghost* entscheidet).
2 Lest das Stück gemeinsam und überlegt, wer welche Rolle spielen soll.
3 Notiert, welche Requisiten und Kostüme ihr benötigt und wie das Bühnenbild aussehen soll.
4 Möchtet ihr Musik oder Geräusche benutzen? Bringt alles mit, was ihr dafür braucht.
5 Probt euer Stück mit den Requisiten, Kostümen und dem Ton, damit ihr euch an alles gewöhnt.
6 Ganz wichtig: Auf der Bühne spricht man laut, langsam und deutlich. Das Publikum möchte euch verstehen.

Die Check out-Seiten helfen dir einzuschätzen, was du schon gut kannst und was du noch üben solltest. Löse die Aufgaben auf dieser Doppelseite und male die Kreise wie auf Seite 20 rot, gelb oder grün aus.

1 Kannst du darüber schreiben, was jemand schon oder noch nicht gemacht hat?
2 Kannst du den Inhalt kurzer Durchsagen auf Deutsch wiedergeben?
3 Kannst du Gegenstände beschreiben?
4 Kannst du Workshopankündigungen verstehen?
5 Kannst du darüber sprechen, was jemand in seinen Ferien vorhat?
6 Kannst du eine Rolle in einer kurzen Theaterszene spielen?

1 grammar: present perfect statements TB p. 190

What have the children done or not done? Complete the sentences with the correct forms.

1 Murad and Kadir ______ (read) a lot of science fiction stories this year.
2 Leo ______ (never be) to a toy museum.
3 Ayla and Erin ______ (just finish) a presentation about Egyptian history.
4 Harry wanted to practise guitar for two hours today, but he ______ (not start, yet).
5 Mrs Smith ______ (travel) a lot and she ______ (meet) interesting people.

Ich kann darüber schreiben, was jemand schon oder noch nicht gemacht hat. ◯

2 audio 3/17

Listen to the announcements and answer the questions.

1 Wann fährt der Zug? ______
2 Was ist im Museum geöffnet? ______
3 Worum geht es in der Ansage? ______
4 Wann schließt der Supermarkt? ______

Ich kann den Inhalt kurzer Durchsagen auf Deutsch wiedergeben. ◯

3

Look at the pictures and complete the text with the words from the box.

at home · birthday · collection · cool · funny · moved · rabbits · says · school · science · text

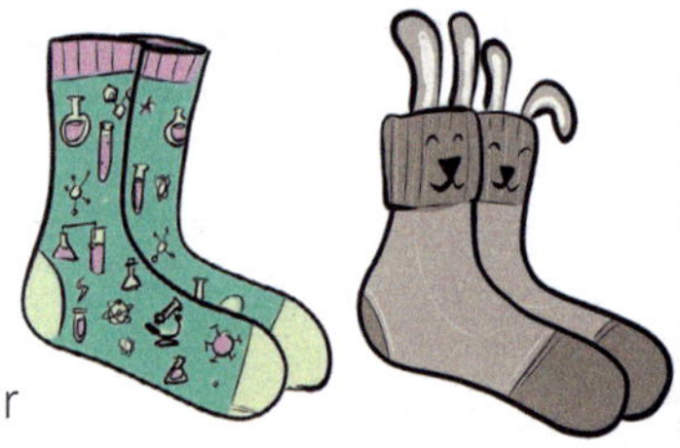

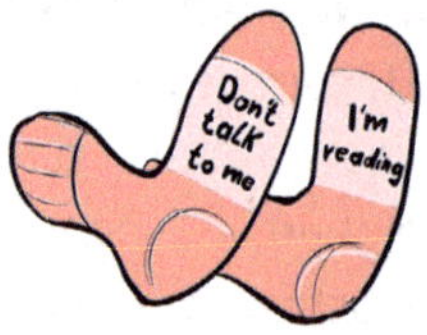

Lily has a large ______ of socks. Some look really ______. Lily's favourite socks are grey and look like ______. Her grandma gave them to her for her last ______. As Lily loves ______, she also has socks with different lab things on them. She often wears them to ______. She has another ______ pair of socks which she only wears ______. She bought them when she ______ to her new room. There is a ______ on them which ______, "Don't talk to me. I'm reading."

Ich kann Gegenstände beschreiben. ◯

4

Read the notes about holiday workshops and tick ✓ the correct sentences.

Cook and taste
Join our cooking club for children at Spitalfields City Farm.
We are going to prepare food from our vegetable garden, cook a healthy meal and eat it together. The food will be free.

Kids rock!
Free three-day music workshop
Try out being in a rock band, practise singing, learn more about DJ skills or find out how to produce music.

All The World's A Circus
Develop on-stage and backstage circus skills. We will practise juggling and acrobatics, but also make some fun props.

1 You have to work in the vegetable garden at the city farm before you start cooking. ☐
2 You don't have to pay for the meal. ☐
3 The music workshop lasts one week. ☐
4 You can play or produce music. ☐
5 At the circus you can learn acrobat skills. ☐
6 You can also learn how to make costumes. ☐

Ich kann Workshopankündigungen verstehen. ◯

5 grammar: going-to future TB p. 192

What are the children going to do in the holidays? Write about their plans.

1 Hamza: visit his aunt and uncle's family in Istanbul

Hamza is going to ____________________

2 Willow and her brother Wayne: spend two weeks at a youth camp in Cornwall

____

3 Finley: take part in a volleyball practice course at his sports club

____

4 Binita: do a one-week bike tour with a group from her youth club

____

Ich kann darüber sprechen, was jemand in seinen Ferien vorhat. ◯

6

Read what Sir Simon says before the ghost inspector arrives. Practise saying his text. Then record your dramatic reading.

Sir Simon:
Oh, I'm sooo nervous! I hope the ghost inspector will think I'm scary. But what will I do if she thinks I'm a bad ghost? *(starts crying)* My life will be really terrible! I will have nowhere to go! Well, let me practise my terrible laughter: Haaa. Haaa. Haaaaa. Mmh, not bad. Now my scary sound: *(loud)* BOO! BOO! BOO! And now some noise: *(shouting)* BANG! BANG! BANG! That's great. *(happy)* I feel better now. I think the inspector will find me really scary.

Ich kann eine Rolle in einer kurzen Theaterszene spielen. ◯

Wenn du noch mehr üben möchtest, gehe zu Practise more – Unit 5. DIGITAL+

Welche der 10 Tipps fandest du in diesem Schuljahr hilfreich? Merke sie dir besonders gut.

Tipp 1 – Unit 1A, 3A, 4A

Bevor du einen Text liest, sieh dir die Überschrift an und überlege, worum es gehen könnte.

Tipp 2 – Unit 2A, 4A

Es gibt viele Wörter, die im Englischen und im Deutschen ähnlich oder sogar gleich sind. Es kann dir helfen, nach solchen Wörtern zu suchen, wenn du einen Text liest.

Tipp 3 – Unit 1A, 2B, 5A

Wenn es zu einem Text Bilder gibt, sieh sie dir an. Sie können dir Hinweise auf den Inhalt des Textes geben.

Tipp 4 – Unit 1B, 3B

Wenn du genaue Informationen aus einem Text herauslesen willst, kannst du ihn gezielt nach und nach durchgehen.
Folgende Fragen können dir helfen:

What? (Was?) Who? (Wer?) When? (Wann?) Where? (Wo?)

Tipp 5 – Unit 4B, 5B

Es kann dir helfen, während des Lesens einen Text durch Unterstreichungen oder Markierungen zu strukturieren. Denke dabei daran, wer spricht oder denkt und achte auf Ortswechsel, Absätze und Sprechblasen.

Tipp 6 – Unit 1B, 4A

Versuche, dir die Wörter, die du beim Lesen nicht gleich verstehst, aus dem Textzusammenhang oder aus der Situation zu erschließen. Nutze dabei nicht nur dein Allgemeinwissen, sondern auch deine sprachlichen Vorkenntnisse.

Tipp 7 – Unit 2B, 3B, 5B

Denke nach, bevor du liest! Oft ist es hilfreich, zu überlegen, was du schon über ein Thema weißt, bevor du einen Text darüber liest. Überlege auch, was du über eine bestimmte Textsorte schon weißt. Was erwartest du z.B. bei einem Rezept, einem Brief oder einer Gespenstergeschichte?

Tipp 8 – Unit 5A

Überfliege einen langen Text zuerst. Sieh dir die Zwischenüberschriften und Bilder an. Dann suche im Text gezielt nach Wörtern und Aussagen *(scan the text)*, die zu den Bildern passen. Du brauchst dabei nicht jedes Wort zu lesen.

Tipp 9 – Unit 3A

Es kann dir helfen, Informationen im Text zu unterstreichen oder zu markieren. Dann kannst du sie beispielsweise in einer Tabelle, einem Diagramm oder einem Wortnetz *(word web)* ordnen.

Tipp 10 – Unit 2A, 4B

Beim Lesen von kürzeren Texten kannst du alle bekannten Wörter unterstreichen. Bei längeren Texten kann es einfacher sein, nur unbekannte Wörter zu unterstreichen. Manchmal erkennst du noch mehr Wörter, wenn du dir den Text anhörst. Alle unbekannten Wörter, die dir wichtig erscheinen, solltest du nachschlagen.

Bildquellen

|Alamy Stock Photo, Abingdon/Oxfordshire: Bell, Graham 7.1; Dewar, Gareth 7.3; Novikov, Sergey 4.1; Vidler, Steve 16.1; Vinogradova, Lilyana 4.2; Wayman, Richard 7.2. |Alamy Stock Photo (RMB), Abingdon/Oxfordshire: Aroon Vater 52.1; Ashley Cooper pics 18.1; frantic 27.1; Kellerman, John 78.1; Langley, Jason 49.1; Paul Brown 25.1. |Bos, Franziska, Frankfurt: 42.1. |iStockphoto.com, Calgary: AlexRaths 27.2; C007 Titel; iStockphoto/RistoArnaudov 78.2; Vesnaandjic 57.1. |Marckwort, Ulf, Kassel: 34.1. |Picture-Alliance GmbH, Frankfurt a.M.: dpa 15.1. |Ruthe, Oda, Braunschweig: 74.1. |Shutterstock.com, New York: FXQuadro 10.1; IrinaK 4.4. |stock.adobe.com, Dublin: Daniel 13.1; ovb64 4.3; streptococcus 15.2.

Videoclips

WB S.10	Track 1 Our summer holidays
WB S.13	Track 2 Planning a day in London
WB S.34	Track 5 Bonfire Night safety tips
WB S.71	Track 11 Past, present or future?

Die Videoclips und Audiotracks wurden gesprochen von

Ben Blake, Brian Bowles, Oliver Brady, Emily Duker, Evie Duker, India Dowers, Naomi Frederick, Max Iveney, Daphne Kouma, Samyar Mahrouyan, Archie Milne, Gina Murray, Chris Nayak, Roisin Rankin, Casey Webb, Ella Webb, George Weightman und Darcey Wilks sowie Schülerinnen und Schüler vom Midhurst Rother College, Midhurst.

DIGITAL+

Alle digitalen Ergänzungen zum Buch erkennst du an dem Symbol **DIGITAL+**.
Dazu zählen auch die Audiotracks und Videoclips.
Gehe auf **www.westermann.de/webcode** und gib den Webcode **WES-128211-001** ein. Du kannst auch den QR-Code scannen.